# TRAPPED!

*Compiled by* Pat Edwards and Wendy Body

## Acknowledgements

We are grateful to the following for permission to reproduce copyright material; the illustrator's agents for four illustrations by Quentin Blake accompanying the poem 'Jack & the Beanstalk' by Roald Dahl in *Revolting Rhymes* by Roald Dahl (pub Puffin); Jonathan Cape Ltd for the poem 'Jack & the Beanstalk' in *Revolting Ryhmes* by Roald Dahl & two accompanying illustrations by Quentin Blake (pub Jonathan Cape Ltd); Faber & Faber Ltd for the poem 'O What is that Sound' in *Collected Poems* by W H Auden & the story 'Miss Piggy' told by Julie Bond in *Dog Days & Cat Naps* by Gene Kemp; the author's agents on behalf of Wanda Finkel for an extract from *The Twilight Province* by George Finkel; C J Fulcher on behalf of the author for the poem 'An Eagle' by Lucy Bassett in *First Year Poetry Anthology 1986-87*, compiled by C J Fulcher, produced by Chepstow Comprehensive School; the author's agents for an extract from *The Hollow Land* by Jane Gardam (pub Puffin Books); Penguin Books Ltd for an extract from *Forbidden Paths of Thual* by Victor Kelleher (pub Kestrel Books, 1979), copyright (c) Victor Kelleher, 1979; Penguin Books Australia Ltd for an extract from *People Might Hear You* by Robin Klein; Scholastic, Inc for an extract from *Avalanche* by Arthur Roth, copyright (c) 1979 by Arthur Roth. Pages 106-7 were written by Wendy Body.

We have been unable to trace the copyright holder in *I Am Fifteen & I Don't Want to Die* by Christine Arnothy (pub 1956) & would appreciate any information that would enable us to do so.

We would like to thank the following for permission to reproduce the photographs: AA Photolibrary, page 107 *below*; Colorsport, pages 106 *above left*, 107 *below centre*; Jersey Museums Service, page 107 *above*; Peter de Sousa, Jersey Photographer, page 107 *above centre*; States of Jersey Tourism, page 106 *above right* and *below*.

Illustrators, other than those acknowledged with each story, include Melissa Webb pp. 26-7; Rolf Heimann pp. 48-9; Rebecca Pannell pp. 50-1; Bruce Rankin p. 86; Peter Foster pp. 94-5; Jenny Beck pp. 106-7.

# Contents

AS THE TWO OF THEM turned away (both limping), Bell and Harry slid forward. Bell eased a huge slab of limestone from a slight dip in the ground, laying bare a hole that might have been a narrow fox-hole lying beneath a shelf of earth and quartz. Then he slid inside it and dropped in to the dark, turning to catch Harry who slid in to the dark beside him.

"Are we down?"

"Aye — but wait till I get — "

"It's not deep."

"Not yet. Wait. Where's the torch?"

"It's a queer smell."

"It gets worse. Nearer the trucks. Like dead bodies. Mind we're not going far. We take a quick look at them trucks and we go straight back. To get back you get on to my shoulders and I jump you up again. Then you lean down in and pull me out after. See?"

"Look." He turned his torch up to the faint light from the blazing day outside, then along the tunnel they stood in. They had dropped through its roof. Stones and rubble lay underfoot. The tunnel went in two directions, each in to deep darkness. The torch, when Bell shone it at the roof picked out small glitters and spangles like frosted cobwebs.

"Is it real silver?"

"I'd say so."

"Already? But we can't be that far down inside?"

"The mines over Alston you can see the silver from the very pit-head. Just by looking through the bars of the grille-thing at the entrance. We went at our school. For History."

"Can we get some? Why did they leave it?"

"Not worth picking out, this lot. The stuff worth having is deep down. Miles down. They used to take folks down there for jaunts in the old days. All dolled-up folks. Rich folks. Used to go down for kicks, wrapped in fancy dust-sheets to see the poor miners slaving away. Used to travel down in the little wagons. Sat on little benches, screaming and hugging each other like in a ghost train."

"Why can't we go down?"

"Don't be soft. It's not maintained now. It's probably all fell in further off. We'd get down there and there'd be a shift and we be gonners. I'se not daft."

"What's a shift?"

"It's what you get round here. Limestone. Ask yon James. It'll be in his book. It was a shift when my grandad flattened his leg. In Light Trees' Home Field. It just suddenly rippled about and threw him down. Like someone moving about under blankets — some giant — he said. Rocks all came tumbling. They call them earthquakes in Japan. Hey — look. Here we are."

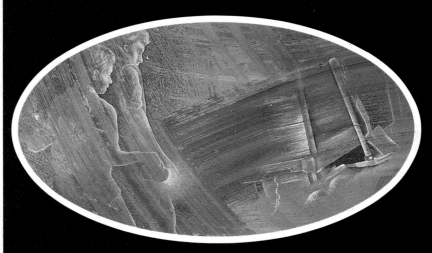

Walking one behind the other, one hand to the tunnel wall and the torch jerking here and there, Bell's foot had come up against something that wasn't rock.

"Here's the rails. Feel."

"They're not wood. They clank."

"They didn't *stay* wood. That was in old ancient times. This mine was in business not that long since. It only stopped when Grandad was a lad. It got too expensive and there was a war and that. Look."

The torch shone on the back of a little wagon. It was attached to another, and another. A little string of them. Propped against the side of one was a fine large pick and a spade.

"Just left here. Just *left*. Look here — "

There were cans and buckets and a couple of spidery, rusty lanterns and two or three tin mugs.

"My — they must have left in a hurry. Fancy leaving all this when they was all poor and going to be out of jobs. What was that?"

5

"What?"

"Noise like a sort of a shower."

"I didn't hear."

"A sort of rumble. Oh!"

From behind them down the tunnel there came a long swishing noise. A sort of sigh, then silence.

"It sounded like water or something," said Harry.

"No. It'll not be water. It's dry enough."

"I've heard your grandad say. 'The drier above — '"

"Aye. I know, ' — the wetter beneath'. But that's the underground rivers. There's no rivers down here. It's a ship-shape mine. It's dry as dry. Look." He shone the torch along the slope of the floor which was dry, though in the two runnels the rails were set in was a thick gluey white liquid like condensed milk.

"I don't like look of yon," said Harry.

Before Bell could correct the yon, there came from down the tunnel a very long and hostile swish and hiss — a sound like a great serpent stirring towards them from the bottom of the mine. Then a thundering long rumble, and a puff of something. They clung to the wagon, and their eyes and noses stung and they began to cough. After what seemed a long time the air cleared, and there was complete silence.

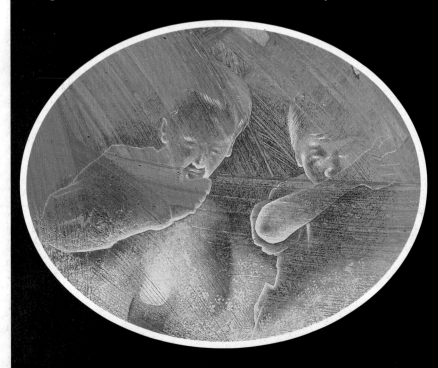

"What was it Bell?"

"We'd best go see."

They walked the little way back again to the hole they had dropped through, feeling the wall as it curved round and slightly down, and came to where they had started out. A solid barrier of earth and rocks completely blocked the tunnel. The hole in the roof, its edges loosened first by them and by the dryness of the earth around, had crumbled and dribbled and showered into the darkness below. First the soil, then smaller stones and then the huge chunks and blocks of rock had settled in tons into the space prepared for them.

There was no sign in the tunnel where five minutes ago they had looked up at the sky that the sun and the grasses and the sheep and the flying grouse were still passing a summer's day hardly ten feet above their heads.

And there was not the least chance in the world of getting out.

Mrs Bateman, back from Penrith with her arms full of clean washing and a lot of parcels, walked into Light Trees' kitchen and called "Harry?"

She looked in the back dairy and saw that the sandwiches for Harry's lunch were still under the pyrex dish and the apples and chocolate lay uneaten beside them. He'll be hungry, she thought, when he does get home. He's been off on the fell a long time. Still. He'll be all right with Bell. Bell knows every inch up there and it's a fine day. No mist to get lost in.

She opened up one of the parcels she had bought in Penrith market and shook out a flannel nightdress with ribbons and lace, and a long apron of white cotton and a sacking apron to wear over it. "Lovely," she said, parading about. "Museum pieces. Lovely." She put on the white apron which had a pinny top and cross-overs at the back. "Florence Nightingale," she said, twisting before the glass hung in the porch. She tied the sacking apron over it. "Now I'm ready to clean out my chicken-houses," she said.

"Silly," she said next, "playing at being someone else. Ridiculous. Just as well I'm alone." She began to unpack the rest of the shopping and the grandfather clock struck five.

"I wonder where he is though?" she said and went and stood on the step and stared about. Then she picked up the field-glasses and went and stood in the Home Field. Through the glasses the fells lay as still and empty as they did through her eyes. "Harry," she called. Her voice echoed. She went in and got the bell she used to ring for Harry to come in for meals when he was smaller and played in the beck, just out of sight.

She kept calling and looking and ringing, but nothing happened. She went in and began to wash salad for supper, thinking that the sacking apron was just the thing for cleaning vegetables. She switched on the radio. She made a pudding. She realised that the radio had been telling her for some time the stock market prices in London and the details of the shipping forecast for the next twenty-four hours, and that listening to it she had been thinking all the time about Harry.

She put down the potato peeler and set off up the fell.

I suppose I could have waited till James came in or Robert got back from London. I'm over anxious. I always was a bore about the children. Silly to worry so. She walked along the dry beck strewn everywhere with whitening thistles and climbed up to the top of the bouse where someone seemed to have been digging lately. A lot of earth had fallen into a deep delve in the fell, with turf torn up and the roots of a may tree sticking up at an angle, feeling the fresh air for the first time since Queen Anne was on the throne. A shift, she thought. A land slip. Like when poor old Mr Hewitson got injured. Quite a big one. Maybe it's subsidence in the old mine. She thought of the honeycombs of rocks beneath her feet, and the rocks, hollow like bones, leading to underground rivers and ball-rooms and cathedrals below, and shuddered. The one thing I'd regret about us coming up here would be if any of them ever took up pot-holing.

She thought for a moment that she heard voices, and stopped. Then she thought she heard a faint metallic hammering noise, very thin and distant. "Kendal says it's haunted up here," she said, and hurried on, and up to the top of the fell where you could see in all directions, right to the Nine Standards, the huge old stones that watched from the horizon.

She stood in the long white apron, shading her eyes.

"Wake up," said Bell, "wake up Harry lad. Here. We've got to yell again."

Harry stirred but didn't wake. Bell shook him. 'Here. Harry. It's late. It must be about night. They'll be looking by now. There's sense yelling now. More sense than before when they was all away."

"My throat's sore."

"It'll be sorer if we're here all night. It's going to get right cold soon. This place has never seen the sun in a million years."

They were behind the iron-barred grille at the entrance to the mine, peering out in to the cave beyond it over the rubbish and rubble of the sixty years since the bars had been fixed. The outer cave mouth was a maddening ten feet away from the inner, barred opening. From the cave mouth the bouse fell steeply away so that you could see the light beyond beginning to change to shadow as it drew to evening. To Bell and Harry it seemed near midnight.

"We ought to start bashing again, too."

"The tin cans and that are wore out."

"There's the pick and shovel. Come on."

Bell began a great assault on the thick iron bars.

"It's killing me ears," said Harry.

"Get to work with that shovel."

Harry made some lesser noises with the shovel. Then they both stopped and cried "Help" for a while.

Then they sat down again and stared at the bars. After a while Harry said, "We'll likely die."

"Get away," said Bell. But dismally. His face was streaked with dirt. It looked gaunt. He kicked the bars with his foot. "By God," he said. "I'se sorry for animals."

"Animals? Sheep could get out. They could ease their way out if they ever wandered in. Dogs could get out. Rabbits could get out. Hares could get out."

"I mean gorillas. Lions and tigers."

"Foxes could get out. Ferrets could get out."

"I mean zoo animals. Caged up. We're caged up. We're caged up like slaves or gorillas. I'll never go near a zoo again."

"Snakes could get out." Harry picked up the end of a chain which hung from the wagon behind him. Already they had tried to heave at the wagons to make them roll up against the iron bars and break the grille down; but it meant pushing up-hill and they were anyway afraid that they might block the entrance altogether and bring down everything. "I'd say we were going to die," Harry said again. He began to feed the chain through the bars. After a bit he had to help it along by jabbing it with the shovel, pushing the shovel sideways through the bars and holding tight to the other end.

"Have you read *Huckleberry Finn*?" asked Bell.

"No."

"Just as well. What you doing?"

"Watching the chain being a snake. Why is it just as well?"

"There was a place like this in *Huckleberry Finn*. Some kids got lost in caves. When they got themselves out — miles away back from the place they'd started, everyone thought they was dead. So all their families blocked up the proper entrance so no other kids could go in again."

"Well I don't wonder at that," said Harry, pressing his face in to the bars and jabbing on at the chain with the shovel end, urging it down the slope towards the cave mouth.

"No, but there was someone else left inside. A terrible Indian. Ages later when someone went up to have another look around, there was this dead skeleton lying, stretching out its poor bony hands. Horrible."

Harry stretched his hands, and his arms, out to their furthest extent through the bars and forced the chain forward a few more links. "Dead skeleton," he said. "That's not so bad. It's live skeletons I don't like."

"Aye. Think of his last hours."

"D'you think these are our last hours?"

"If we don't get clanking and shouting again they are. Go on. Get clanking that shovel against the bars again. Gis hold of the pick and I'll have a thrust at that chain."

After the morning's thistling Old Hewitson had gone off down Quarry Hill with his scythe over his shoulder like Old Father Time, and James alongside. They waited a while on the wooden bridge in the village for Kendal the sweep. When Kendal's land-rover appeared Old Hewitson, James and the scythe were all installed in it and the land-rover turned and made for a remote farmhouse on Stainmore where propped against the yard wall there stood a large brass bed.

The two ends of the bed and the metal base had been lifted in to the land-rover and then everyone had gone in to the farm house for tea.

This had taken a very long time, for there was a lot to talk about — there is always more to talk about in places where not much seems to happen — and the farmer and his wife did not set them over the yard to the land-rover again to say good-bye and thank them for taking the bed off their hands until after five o'clock.

Then there had to be another long talk from the steering wheel and by the time they eventually rattled off and reached the village, it was time for the stock market prices and the shipping forecast had they been interested in either.

Through the village they went and up Quarry Hill past Light Trees and as far as the culvert bridge over the dry beck.

"Now's the problem," said Kendal, "how to get the bed up the fell."

"I thistled this place this morning," said Old Hewitson. "We might see if it'll run along the beck bottom."

The land-rover lumbered down the bank and into the stream bed. It took its way along with the two old men now and then hitting their heads on the land-rover roof, and James constantly holding his shin. "Good for the liver," said Kendal.

"Not good for the bed," said Old Hewitson. "It's making music like the Sally Army."

They passed the foot of the bouse, where James's Geology book still lay surveying the evening sky, and turned the corner at the bottom of the cleft and the broken wire fence. They lifted down the bed, removed the old wire from the gap and fastened the bed-ends and the metal base across the dry beck.

"Fits a treat," said Old Hewitson. "Very handsome. No need to mention it to the authorities."

"Last a hundred years," said Kendal, "and very interesting it looks. Just the thing for an Area of Outstanding Natural Beauty. Hello."

"What?"

"Did you hear something?"

They stood. The evening, gentle with the warmth of the long day smelled of gorse and wild thyme and a hundred miles of clean turf. Through the silence came a faint sound of metal, rhythmically hammering from the top of the bouse, and thin and strange lamenting cries.

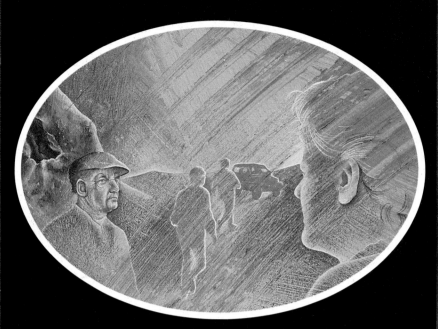

At the same moment Mrs Bateman in her long apron paced in to view and stood mournfully shading her eyes and looking in to the distance.

James gave a scream and fled, kicking aside his Geology book and vanishing in to the sunset.

He was closely followed by Kendal who made for the land-rover, shouting wildly to Old Hewitson to follow him, and starting the engine.

Only Old Hewitson — and Mrs Bateman — stood their ground, and only Old Hewitson saw something come in to view in queer jerks at the top of the bouse and watched a rusty and enormous chain emerge from what looked like the very earth itself, gather speed, slide lumpily forward, drop through the air and fall at last at his own uneven feet.

"Turn that car, Kendal," he cried. "Get that James back here. Mrs Bateman, stay up there on the bouse. We're in for a hard evening. It's going to take the lot of us."

"And for my part," said Mr Teesdale at past ten o'clock at night, "I'd a mind to leave them there."

"And mine," said Mr Bateman in his London suit which was not looking its best.

"Sitting there like two fond monkeys. Deserved nuts and water for a week."

"Beyond me. Beyond me," said Mr Bateman.

"I just couldn't believe — I couldn't believe it," said Mrs Bateman. "All I did was appear and everyone screamed and scattered. Ghost! Do I look like a ghost?"

"Yes," said Eileen, Bell's sister, "you did. I seed it once. I seed that ghost when I was just about to be a teen-ager. Just before you're teen-age you see ghosts easiest. I read it in a magazine. Just before you're teen-age you're very psychic and impressionable."

"I'd give Bell psychic and impressionable," said his father.

"I'd not call that Kendal teen-age," said Mrs Bateman, "at least not in years."

"I saw no ghosts," said Bell, "I was that busy getting us out."

"Getting us out?" said Harry. "You was going on about dead skeletons and terrible Indians. Who got the chain moving?"

"Aye, well you did. I'll say that."

"A pair of loonies," said James.

"Who went running?" said Harry. "Ghosts of dead miners. Dead miners' mothers! And you a scientist."

"That lad of Meccers never got lost up the mines anyway," said Mrs Teesdale, "I heard tell he took off to South America and got to be a millionaire."

"It was still very dreadful for his mother," said Mr Bateman.

"Tell me when it ever isn't," said Mrs Bateman, collapsed on the Light Trees' sofa, still in her aprons. "Tell me when it ever isn't."

"When they're safe home," said Grandad Hewitson. "Give thanks. They're safe home. And both of them a bit wiser than when the sun rose up this morning."

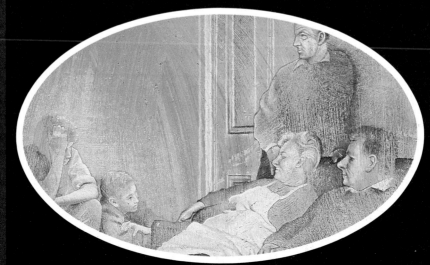

15

Written by Jane Gardam                    Illustrated by Paul Hunt

# GET ME OUT OF HERE!

*When 14 year old Chris Palmer decides to shoot a coyote while out skiing, he has no idea that the crack of his rifle will start an avalanche — an avalanche that will bury Chris in an icy tomb. He pins his hopes on the belief that his parents and brother, Terry, will remember that he planned to ski up to Frenchman's Flats.*

"I'm drowning! I'm drowning!" Chris was struggling back to consciousness. No matter how hard he worked his lungs, he couldn't seem to get enough air. He sucked in desperately, then threw back his head and screamed. "Help me, somebody! Help me!" He tried frantically to claw himself free from the snow.

The panic passed as soon as he realized his screams were doing no good. Forcing himself to calm down, he took stock of his situation. His arms and legs were held tight, but he could rock his head back and forth.

He set to work to clear more space around his face. Soon he was able to push back and look upward through the dim gray light that filtered down. High above, perhaps six feet over his head, he could see a small round hole through which poured a ray of bright sunshine. Above the hole a patch of blue was visible.

"The sky!" he cried out. "I can see the sky!"

The sight lifted his spirits. He felt a flood of gratitude. He had a pipeline to the surface air. The sun must have melted through a thin spot in the snow cover. And just in time too; he could not have lasted much longer in the oxygen-poor air of his prison.

But how long could he survive? He realized he had to have three things: food, water, and air. For the moment he had air. For water he could bite out a few mouthfuls of snow and melt them. He hadn't brought

17

any food, but with plenty of air and water he could last a few days at least. The big problem was that no one knew where he was. His family wouldn't start looking for him until late afternoon at the earliest. Perhaps they might even wait until the following morning before they began their search. They knew he had gone to Frenchman's Flats. From there they would pick up his ski tracks leading to Hidden Lake.

Even if they waited until morning, they should reach the avalanche site by tomorrow afternoon at the latest. As soon as they reached the snowslide, they would know what had happened. They would work through the piled-up masses of snow with their poles, probing for his body. All he had to do was hang on for twenty-four hours. The thought sent another wave of panic over him, and he began to shudder. Then he went rigid, biting his lip until he finally got control of his fear. If he was going to last twenty-four hours in this snow cell, he would have to control his hysteria.

If he had only taken the sandwiches and coffee Mom had offered him. If he had only turned back when he reached Frenchman's Flats. If he had only not seen that coyote. Or not shot at it. If he had only not gone skiing this morning. If only . . . if only . . .

Chris felt another shudder run through his body. His nerves were strung taut. Curious, he thought, that so far he had not really felt the cold. Of course he was well sheltered from any wind, and he supposed the snow also acted as a sort of insulation. His body heat probably warmed up the air around him, at least enough to keep him from freezing. Except perhaps for his feet. He just hoped that they wouldn't get frost-bitten.

He tried to bend from the waist, to lever the upper half of his body forward a couple of inches. It was difficult to move — still, he could be worse. Suppose he had ended up stretched out on his back! Or had come to rest upside down! He couldn't have lasted even an hour then. At least being upright gave him some sort of a chance.

He bent again at the waist and tried to rock back and forth. After half an hour's hard rocking around the upper half of his body, he managed to compress enough snow to add another couple of inches clearance.

18

Suddenly anxious about the air hole, he tilted back his head to look up. The sunlight was more slanting now. The sun had passed its meridian. It was already afternoon. He wondered what time it was. He had a digital watch, but unless he could free his arms there was no way he could see it. There was a possibility that he could work his arms loose, but there was still no way he could free his legs with the skis so firmly bound to his feet. It was hopeless. The best thing was not to struggle, to save his strength and hope that he could last until someone reached him tomorrow.

Perhaps he should try to sleep for a while. He might have to do a lot of shouting tomorrow, and he ought to save his strength until he was sure that people were nearby and searching for him.

He closed his eyes and his thoughts turned to his family. What would they think when he didn't come home? Suppose he died. How would Mom and Dad take it? And Terry, how would he react? Old Terry would miss him, but wouldn't he also be a bit relieved? There wouldn't be anyone else whose grades they would hold up to him for comparison. And Terry would have the whole bedroom to himself. He could fill the walls on Chris's side of the room with all kinds of sports charts.

Chris tried to will himself to sleep. Instead of counting sheep, he went over some of the lines in the play. He thought of Hamlet's death speech. How did it go? Slowly he began to recite: *"Oh I die, Horatio*, something, something. *I cannot live to hear the news of England . . ."*

The words moved him as they had never moved him before in any of the rehearsals. Then he remembered Horatio's final words: *"Now cracks a noble heart. Good night sweet Prince and flights of angels sing thee to thy rest."*

Chris's eyes filled with tears, and he began furiously to rock his body back and forth, trying to struggle out of his snow tomb.

"Get me out of here!" he yelled, over and over again.

"They'll find me, first thing in the morning they're sure to find me," Chris said aloud. It was full night now — blackness, like blindness, everywhere. The night hours would be the worst, he knew. He was sure that the snow was going to collapse down around his head and smother him.

"They'll find me. They'll find me, all right," he said again and again
into the darkness. "Eeeny meeny miney mo!" he sang aloud. "They will
find me in the snow!" To block out thoughts of smothering and to keep
his mind busy, he began to do mathematical problems in his head. After
that he recited all the Spanish words he knew. Then he sang all the
songs he knew. He was even able to grin at the thought of a passerby
walking over the air hole and hearing singing deep within the snow.

Through the worst parts of the night, Chris held on to one thought: His
folks were organizing a rescue team. By first light in the morning at least
a dozen people would be out searching for him. All he had to do was
hang on for another few hours. By noon, at the latest, someone would
reach him.

Toward morning the air in his snow prison turned bad again. For periods of five minutes or more, Chris found himself panting strenuously. Despite all the snow around him, he felt hot and wondered if he was running a fever. That was all he needed, he groaned, to come down with pneumonia or some illness like that.

Gradually the blackness around him turned gray and he was able to make out the walls of his prison. The first thing that struck him was that he had more space immediately above his head. His body had settled a good six inches during the night, faster than the surrounding snow was settling. There was also more clear space around his arms and shoulders. The settling snow had drawn away from him somewhat.

He looked up, but he couldn't see his air hole. Perhaps it was still too early. Was the sun not up yet? He had no way of knowing the time. He had still not been able to free his arms to look at his wristwatch.

He started moving his left shoulder up and down, trying to clear more space. Then he doubled up his left hand, made a fist, and punched downward. Half a dozen punches and he could feel a definite cracking of the icy shield that had formed around his body during the night.

He took a rest then and thought about what he was doing. He was going about things the wrong way, he decided. He ought to free his best arm — his right arm — first. Then he could use that arm to reach across to his left hip, and get his hunting knife. With the hunting knife out, he could carve more space for himself. He could even free his left arm and finally get to his watch.

Rejuvenated by this plan of action, he began moving his right arm up and down, fanning his elbow in and out, like a wing, and moving his shoulder back and forth. It took a lot of work, but a last desperate wriggle of the right side of his body loosened his arm. Suddenly his right hand was up and in front of his face.

He was so excited, he almost cried. It was as though a familiar friend had come to pay him a visit and share his problems. He pulled the leather mitten off with his teeth, then repeated the operation with the inner wool glove. The glove and mitten he stuck inside the neck of his jacket.

His hand might be numb and half frozen, but it looked beautiful. He stared at the long, slender fingers, the nails smoothly rounded, the thumb perfectly shaped. He waggled the fingers a bit and spoke to the hand. "Hello, hand!" The hand nodded back to him, patted his cheeks, his nose, his lips. Then he squirmed the hand down inside his wool shirt and undershirt and let it nest in the hollow of his left armpit.

While he was warming his hand, he leaned back and looked up. He still couldn't locate the opening. Puzzled, he stared up at the cone of snow for a moment before the fact fully struck home. The air hole was blocked! It must have snowed again during the night!

Chris dropped his head and groaned with despair. He should have realized. It had been getting harder to breathe, but he assumed it was because of all his physical activity. Now it was evident that not enough air was filtering down to him.

Before he could do anything about it, though, he had to relieve himself. He was really in pain. He pushed his hand down through the snow, found the tab of his zipper, and unzipped his pants. He wrinkled his nose at the harsh smell that rose from his urine. That didn't help to make the air any purer. One thing it did do, though — it melted away some of the snow around his legs.

When he was through, he zipped up his pants and put the glove and mitten back on. He used his teeth as a vise as he worked each finger into its individual compartment. Then he snaked his his hand up in front of his face, stretching the arm and hand and fingers as high as they would go. In this way he managed to make a narrow tunnel up through the snow.

Unfortunately, he was still short of the surface, a good three or four feet, he guessed. If he could only get to his knife, he could extend his upward reach another six inches or so. But that would still leave him a couple of feet short of breaking through. If he had only held on to one of his ski poles. Or if only he had a breathing tube that he could poke up through the snow and into the air above. He had read that Indians used to hide from their enemies in creeks and rivers that way. They would sink themselves under the water and use a hollow reed, sticking above the surface, to breathe through.

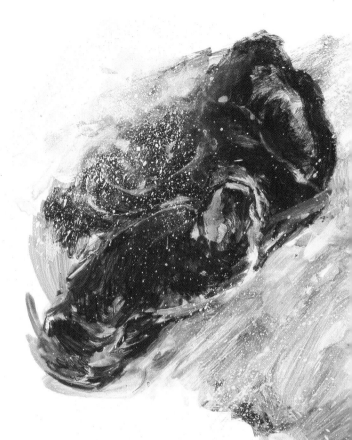

As the air got worse, he grew sleepy. But he was afraid to close his eyes for fear he would go into a coma. Above all, he wanted to stay awake until noon. By then he expected someone to find him.

He began to drift off. It was so hard to keep his eyes open. Maybe he should try to free his left arm and get to his watch. He thrust his hand inside his jacket and let his head drop to his chest. He would just close his eyes for a second or so. A five-minute nap surely wouldn't do any harm . . .

When he woke up, he was patting the snow in front of his face. For a moment he was disoriented. Then with a terrible sense of despair, he realized where he was. He was like a condemned man in jail who dreams of an earlier, happier time when he was free, then wakes up to the knowledge that he has only a few days to live.

Chris wasn't with his family — that was a dream. He was all by himself in the mountains, trapped under tons of snow, with perhaps only hours to live if help didn't reach him soon.

He leaned back and looked up. His bitter disappointment on waking up was lessened by the sight of a tiny ray of sunshine. His surface pocket was open again, and the air smelled cool and fresh. The fresh air was probably what woke him. Now if he could just find a way to keep this life-line open through the snow-banked roof.

He forced his right hand downward and across the front of his waist. He would get to his hunting knife and try to free his other arm. It was only then that he realized the full significance of that fall of snow during the night. His ski tracks were now covered with fresh snow. His rescuers had no way of tracking him!

"Oh no!" he moaned. "No! No! No! That's not fair!"

---

Arthur Roth
*Illustrated by* Pat Sirninger

---

# I CAN'T FEEL MY TOES!

Almost everybody, at some stage, has experienced the deliciously strange sensation of numbness or tingling in the lower legs, feet or toes, and even hands. Next time it happens to you, stop and briefly observe how you're sitting when it occurs.

Sitting in cramped positions can affect the circulation of your blood, especially if you already have poor circulation to begin with.

**Were you kneeling?**

**Sitting cross-legged?**

**Sitting on your hands?**

## What do we mean by 'circulation'?

'Circulation' refers to the passage of blood that is pumped through the heart and out again via a network of blood vessels. (I wonder if the blood ever becomes confused about which direction it should be taking?). The blood vessels carry the oxygen-rich blood to all the tissues in the body. On its return journey, the blood carries the carbon dioxide back from the body's cells. Because the cells have removed most of the oxygen from it, it's now described as 'deoxygenated'.

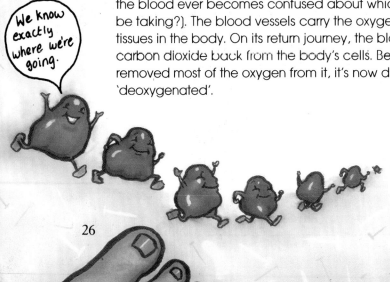

**We know exactly where we're going.**

The blood goes back to the heart and out again to the lungs where it is — wait for it — reoxygenated. Phew! And, after all this, it returns to the heart and repeats its circular journey. The wonderful thing is it never stops; at least not while your heart is still pumping. Without this marvellous piece of design and engineering, our bodies would be starved of oxygen and valuable nutrients and would be full of nasty waste products. In fact, we'd be pretty sick.

## What about cold noses and 'toeses'?

In cold weather, our internal body temperature can drop, particularly if we don't exercise, eat warming food or wear warm clothing. When this happens, the skin blood vessels will shrink or constrict. Blood flow to the surface of the body is lessened as the body tries to keep the more important parts of itself warm, like the brain. Hence, your brain will get blood at the expense of your fingers, ears, noses and 'toeses'! Perhaps there is a hidden message in that old-fashioned saying 'Wear a hat to warm your toes'.

Didn't you know you can lose a lot of heat through the top of your head?

- In the western world, our thanks go to William Harvey who first discovered the circulation of the blood in 1628.
- In the eastern world, the Chinese had known about the circulation of the blood many centuries earlier.

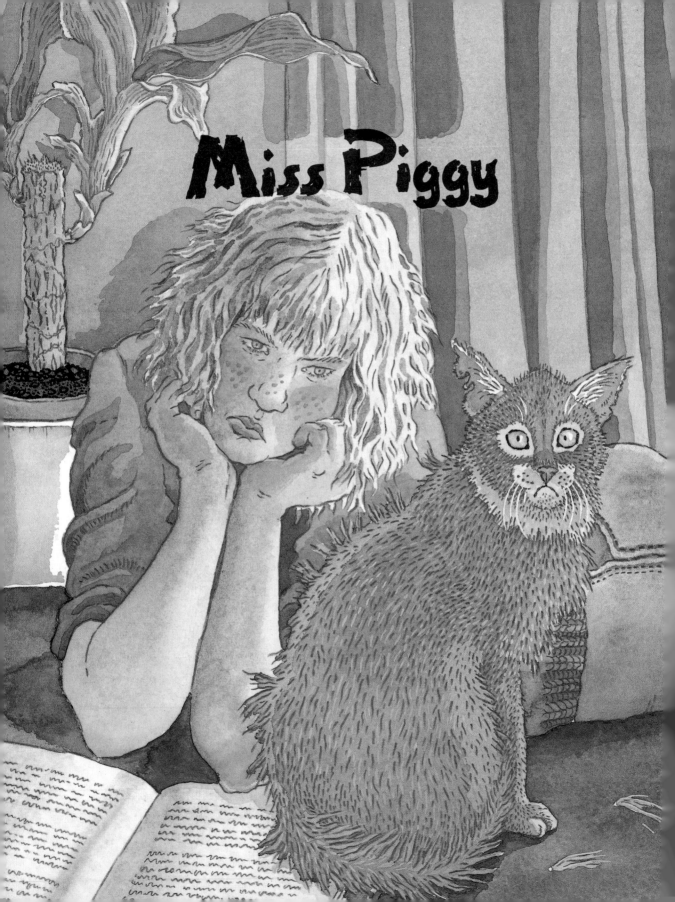

Miss Piggy
*told by Julie Bond*

It must be wonderful to own an animal that you are proud of, a dog, say, that could frighten the fiercest burglar or even our Head-teacher, Mrs. Potts, just about the two most scary possibles I can think of. Imagine strolling gently through the park with a Great Dane or an Alsatian. If I had a dog like that I wouldn't have to hide behind the dusty old laurel bushes with my friends, Jason and Yasmine, when Merv Tucker and gang are looking for trouble and threatening to duff us up. He's known as the Iron Boy because he's so tough.

If I had a dog, a big dog, I think I'd call him Max.

"Show them, Max," I'd whisper to him, and Max would open his giant jaws, and snarl, and Merv Tucker and his gang would run away, squawking with terror, and I'd pretend to undo his lead, and they'd go even faster, home to their mothers.

Actually, I wouldn't dare undo a dog's lead in the park, as the park keeper is very hot on dogs being properly on their leads, and is always on the lookout for offenders, popping out from behind trees and under wheelbarrows when you least expect him, and I do not think he likes Yasmine and Jason and me much, after that time when Chilli — that's Jason's dog — got into the prize flower-bed. Chilli is a lovely dog, a tall, thin, sad red setter, and so gentle that if a burglar came through the window with a sack full of safe-breaking apparatus and two revolvers, she would wag her tail, lick him all over his face and pant *welcome*. It does seem to be our luck to have animals like that. Animals that are timid. Yasmine has twenty white mice, and they are extra timid even for white mice. I think this is sad, and that perhaps it's because our animals are like us, not very brave, not brave at all, really.

But even if that is so, I am not as awful as Miss Piggy. And I do hope that you are not taken in by this name.

No, it is not the famous and terrible television star that I am talking about. Miss Piggy is our cat, and my mother says no, I can't have another animal for a pet, not when I already have Miss Piggy. But I should very much like to have another animal, almost anything would do rather than that cat. My brother gave her that name. He's into punk and way-out humour, and he called her Miss Piggy for two reasons, he says — one, she's the ugliest cat he ever saw, and two, she's the stupidest . . .

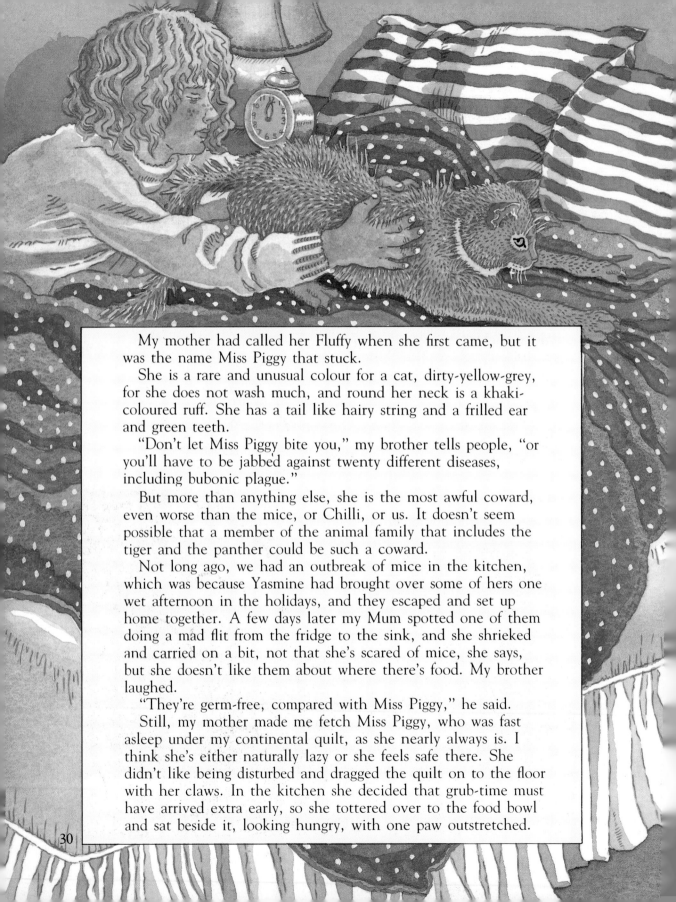

My mother had called her Fluffy when she first came, but it was the name Miss Piggy that stuck.

She is a rare and unusual colour for a cat, dirty-yellow-grey, for she does not wash much, and round her neck is a khaki-coloured ruff. She has a tail like hairy string and a frilled ear and green teeth.

"Don't let Miss Piggy bite you," my brother tells people, "or you'll have to be jabbed against twenty different diseases, including bubonic plague."

But more than anything else, she is the most awful coward, even worse than the mice, or Chilli, or us. It doesn't seem possible that a member of the animal family that includes the tiger and the panther could be such a coward.

Not long ago, we had an outbreak of mice in the kitchen, which was because Yasmine had brought over some of hers one wet afternoon in the holidays, and they escaped and set up home together. A few days later my Mum spotted one of them doing a mad flit from the fridge to the sink, and she shrieked and carried on a bit, not that she's scared of mice, she says, but she doesn't like them about where there's food. My brother laughed.

"They're germ-free, compared with Miss Piggy," he said.

Still, my mother made me fetch Miss Piggy, who was fast asleep under my continental quilt, as she nearly always is. I think she's either naturally lazy or she feels safe there. She didn't like being disturbed and dragged the quilt on to the floor with her claws. In the kitchen she decided that grub-time must have arrived extra early, so she tottered over to the food bowl and sat beside it, looking hungry, with one paw outstretched.

"Get that mouse," ordered my mother. Miss Piggy looked back at her. It was obvious that the word "mouse" meant nothing to her, and, anyway, it had disappeared by now.

"Try catching your meals for a change," Mum went on, bitterly.

At that moment a twitching nose and long white whiskers appeared from behind an ironing-board in the corner.

"Get it," Mum yelled, hopping, and then, "Go on, chase them out of here!" for another one ran suddenly straight under the table and towards Miss Piggy. (Yasmine's mice are a bit stupid, I think.) The sight of a mouse rushing straight for her was just too much for Miss Piggy. With a yowl of terror, she leapt up on to a chair and stood there, trembling. My brother moved fast, grabbed both the mice in turn by their tails, swung them wickedly towards Miss Piggy, who nearly fell off the chair in fright, then popped them into a nearly empty cornflake packet and gave it to me.

"Your mate Yasmine might like these for her collection," he said, and winked.

"You ought to be ashamed of yourself, Miss Piggy," said Mum. "Fancy being afraid of two harmless little mice."

"What about you, Mum?" I thought, but didn't say.

The other day Miss Piggy did have an unusual fit of energy and chased a sparrow across the garden, which made a change as normally they chase her. The bird got away, of course, but in the meantime she had scrambled up a fruit-tree, a small apple-tree, so tiny that if I swing on the lowest branch my knees hit the ground. And there that cat sat, trembling, on this low branch, eyes screwed tight shut.

"There you are," I said to Yasmine and Jason. "You see. Not only is she afraid of mice, she's afraid of heights, as well."

"Vertigo," said Jason. He always knows words like that.

"I don't care what it's called, it's not right for a cat. Cats are supposed to be fearless hunters, leaping about on roofs and fighting. Put her on a roof and she'd drop off from sheer terror."

"Perhaps she's already lost eight of her nine lives and is taking good care of the last one," said Yasmine, lifting her down and making clucking noises, meant to comfort, I think, but sounding like a hen with hiccups. "Cowards can't help being cowards," she went on. She is a kind girl.

Those words came back to my mind when we took Chilli for her walk that evening, for who should appear but Merv, looking more like the Iron Boy than ever, with all his gang with him and a DOG. Paul Brickley, the gang's Number Two, was holding it with a chain as thick as its middle. This DOG had more teeth than I have ever seen on one animal other than a crocodile, and it was smiling generously with them. In size it was somewhere between a wolf and a pony. Merv prodded me in the chest, which I have never liked.

"Look at that, Jool. Just you take a look at that. That, you gotter admit, really looks like . . . a DAWG."

I admitted it. There wasn't much else I could do, as Paul Brickley was holding it so that it towered all over me, dribbling evilly. Merv prodded me again.

"Not much like that . . . thing . . . you've got there, is it?"
He turned me with an Iron Hand so that I could see Chilli,
who was sniffing a dandelion.

"Not much of a dawg, is it? You gotter admit it."

I admitted it again, as dreams of my huge Great Dane or
Alsatian called Max withered and died away for ever.

"And so," continued Merv, "you lot, keep out of our way,
see? Or you and that grotty animal there will feel the weight
of my fist."

He showed me the fist, clenched into bony lumps, then Paul
showed me the dog's teeth, with saliva dribbling all over them.
Then the gang went on its sunshiny way. We headed for
home, not saying much. There didn't appear to be much to
say.

"Cheeky lot," said Yasmine, at last, bravely. "I wanted to
hit Merv."

I wanted to ask what had stopped her, but I didn't. I hadn't
shown up very well either. 'Cowards can't help being cowards'
kept going through my head, but it didn't comfort me much.

Spring came, at last. Blossom sprang out on the trees and bushes, flowers bloomed, birds built nests, children went tadpoling. My brother found three new girlfriends. We discovered a place, a secret place, a hut in the corner of the allotments (we never went to the park, nowadays) and it was sheltered by a tall hedge, now covered with fat, green, bursting buds. No one took any notice of us or told us not to go there, so after a time we did it up a bit, with mats and boxes. Chilli liked it, flopping her long body over the floor like a red rug. Yasmine brought one of her cages, and a couple of mice, and then one evening Miss Piggy turned up, purring like a rusty engine as she settled down.

"She won't hurt the mice, will she?" asked Yasmine.

"Don't be daft," I said, fiddling with the old transistor my brother had given me.

But one night we came to find the hut wrecked, comics torn up, the carpet thrown among the nettles, and food scattered. Yasmine had always taken the mice back home with her each night, which was a good thing, as the cage had been flung on the floor and the mouse-wheel wrecked. As we were trying to clean up the door was crashed open.

"Out, out, you lot!" shouted Merv. Paul, gang and the DOG were right behind him. "We're doing a takeover."

'Cowards can't help being cowards' ran through my brain again. Fat lot of good, that was. I wanted to push in Merv's beastly grinning face, to scream and shout and kick, but there were too many in the gang and they were bigger than us. It wasn't fair, it wasn't fair. We'd found the hut first, made it cosy, done it up. It was ours. Our place. And they were taking it, spoiling it, as they spoilt everything.

And like a hawk dropping from the sky on to a rabbit, down from the roof dropped Miss Piggy, right on to Merv's head, digging in her claws to hang on. Part of me thought, she's got it all wrong as usual, she thinks he's a rug or something like that. And he was yelling blue murder, so Miss Piggy dug in even deeper, as she hates loud noises, they make her nervous.

"Get it off! Get it off! Help!"

Paul's dog was snarling and tugging. Paul could hardly hold
him. This frightened Miss Piggy even more, and she gave a
terrible wail and launched herself on to its head, digging her
claws right in. The dog howled a dreadful, dismal howl, and
rushed off along the path, pulling Paul flat on his face and
dragging him along over the rough ground. Then across the
newly planted allotments rushed the dog madly, with Miss
Piggy on his head, like a circus performer.

"Get those animals off the gardens!" went up the cry, and
several gardeners joined in the chase. Paul had let go of the
lead by now. Two of the gang went to him and two more tried
to help Merv, who was feeling his head to see if it was still all
there.

Yasmine, Jason and I, we looked at each other. Our time
had come. The moment had arrived. We weren't cowards. No,
not us.

We rushed at them, arms waving, feet kicking.

"Get out! Get out! It's our hut. Don't come here again!"

Even Chilli staggered to her feet and woofed at them, and
then lay down again. How the gang ran. Like lightning.

They leave us alone these days. No one interferes with the hut. A rumour went around that Miss Piggy was gifted with magic powers, enabling her to get terrible revenge on anyone who offended her. I think my brother started it, at least he had a very funny look on his face when I told him this. Besides, though I don't think anyone else saw him, I know he was behind the hut with Anna Spence, his latest, that evening. Though he said, when I asked, that no, he didn't throw Miss Piggy over the roof on to Merv Tucker's head. But then you can never tell what he means or doesn't mean, 'cos of this way-out humour I told you about.

The funny thing is, though, that although I know Miss Piggy wasn't really being brave, she hasn't been so cowardly since. Yesterday she was chasing quite a large bird, a pigeon. Yasmine and Jason don't look quite so mouselike, either. And Chilli is going to have puppies. Me? Oh, well, I was never so much of a coward as the others, anyway.

Written by Gene Kemp
Illustrated by Sara Woodward

# THEY WON'T LET ME OUT!

When her Aunt Loris marries the forbidding Mr Tyrell, 12 year old Frances is introduced to the mysterious Temple with its strange, fanatical beliefs. All its adherents seem convinced that a terrible war will soon break out, killing everyone but those who belong to the Temple. Their lives are governed by secrecy — no one must ever divulge the Temple's whereabouts. Children are educated at home, living behind locked doors, always afraid of discovery by the authorities.

Within the Tyrell household, Frances finds herself desperately missing her friend, Kerry, and the wonderful ordinariness of life outside. She finds it hard to believe that the Tyrell girls, Rosgrana, Helen and Claire have no knowledge of even simple pleasures, like going shopping, watching TV or walking on a beach. To please her aunt, she tries to fit in and to be a "worthy" member of the Temple, but soon she rebels and, when her new uncle decides that she has to be sent to a special school to be re-educated so that she accepts totally this new religion, Frances decides that she must escape at all costs. On a piece of stolen notepaper she writes a plea for help, asking whoever finds her letter to contact Kerry's mother, and carries it round with her waiting for an opportunity to throw it over the back fence.

Meanwhile, Claire has fallen dangerously ill . . .


Claire was in obvious pain and her eyes were set in large dark rings. In spite of the chill in the room, her nightgown was damp with sweat. She moved her head fretfully on the pillows and peered at Frances, and through her, seeing nothing. Frances, nudged by fear, backed away and fled to the kitchen. "Claire's looking terrible!" she cried. "She's breathing funny and you've got to get a doctor for her."

"Stop raising your voice like that," Rosgrana said angrily.

"I should have thought you'd be the one yelling, making him do something to help her. She's your sister. She's never going to get better, just lying up there."

"The arrangements of this house have nothing to do with you," Rosgrana said. "And if you can't behave and speak quietly, you're going to have to stay down in the storeroom until they come to get you tomorrow."

"It wouldn't matter which room I was in," Frances said. "What's so different about the rest of the house, anyway? It's all part of the same prison." Her fingers closed upon the letter which she had transferred to her dress pocket. Her expression changed from belligerence to cunning. She would throw the letter over the fence and the people next door would come and attend to the appalling nightmare that was the Tyrells' way of life. Tonight she would be sleeping at Kerry's house. "Do you want those sheets hung up on the line?" she asked.

"Yes. You'd be better employed offering help with the work than in being impertinent," Rosgrana said coldly, and unlocked the back door.

Frances carried out the laundry basket. She carefully pegged up two sheets and, using them as a screen, ran to the fence and tossed the weighted letter over. She heard the soft thud of its landing and hurried back to the clothesline. Struggling with another wet, heavy sheet, she glanced up at the window belonging to Helen's bedroom, and thought of the scratch lines. If she scraped away enough of the paint, she'd be able to look down into the yard next door and watch those people find her letter.

"It shouldn't have taken so long to hang up a few sheets," Rosgrana scolded, letting her in and relocking the door. "They won't tolerate that sort of laziness when you're living at the temple. Nobody will make allowances for you there. If you want to be accepted and come back here to live, you're going to have to alter your ways."

"I don't want to be accepted," Frances said. She looked at the packed suitcase, standing in readiness at the foot of the stairs. When the people next door found her letter and came in to take her away, she would leave it where it was. It was packed with all those neat, sad-coloured clothes. At Kerry's, she would borrow a pair of jeans and go for a walk somewhere, where she could yell and laugh and make as much noise as she liked.

She ran upstairs to Helen's room. Helen had stacked some books in front of the window, to conceal the scratched paint. Frances shoved them aside and began to enlarge the scratches. "Those people could be reading the letter right now," she thought. "They'll come and ring at the door, and this time Rosgrana won't be able to get away with pretending there's no one home. Those people will break the door down if they have to."

She scraped away flakes of paint into a coin-sized hole, large enough to look out and see where her letter lay, waiting to be picked up. "You're not to touch that window again!" Helen said from the doorway. "I covered it up so they wouldn't find out. Rosgrana is going to be watching what you do every minute until they take you to the temple tomorrow morning. They know you can't be trusted."

"I won't be going to the temple," Frances said triumphantly. "I fixed it so I wouldn't have to."

She bent and looked through the hole in the paintwork. There was a clear view over the fence into the property next door. She could see quite plainly where her message lay, like a bright arrowhead, on a patch of grass on the other side of the tall fence. Her aim had been true, and the message hadn't been snared up in bushes where nobody could find it. It was there in full view, just waiting for someone to come and pick it up.

And it was quite apparent that nobody would come. Ever. There was no house set in a garden next door, no neighbours. She looked down into a vacant block choked with blackberries and old dumped cars and ancient rubbish. Her letter lay in a little clearing in the middle of undergrowth so dense and thick that it was quite obvious that nobody had walked in there for a long time. The Tyrell house stood all by itself, quite alone, set in the framework of the street, the back lane, the alleyway, and the rubbish-strewn vacant block. And that was what her message was now, rubbish consigned to a dumping ground.

"I could have spared you the trouble of making that hole," Helen said. "I could have told you there was nothing to look at from this window. That block of land has always been like that."

Frances couldn't answer, grieving for Kerry and a world where the sun gilded the surface of an ocean. She mourned for her aunt, who had locked them both into this barren life. And for Helen, who had never walked along a beach.

"Don't look like that," pleaded Helen. "Just be well behaved at the temple and don't argue with them, and do as they say. They might let me see you, when we come there for meetings. It's for your own good, Frances. I want you to be safe when the war comes, being one of us."

Claire was whimpering from the little room at the top of the stairs. "I must go back to her," Helen said helplessly. "They told me I have to sit with her. She's so ill that Father arranged for someone to come and examine her this afternoon. I have to stay with her until he comes."

Frances kept her face turned away so Helen couldn't decipher the sudden rush of renewed hope. It didn't matter at all that there was nobody to come along and find that message; she was going to get out of the house anyway. She would walk out of that house with the doctor who was coming to look at Claire. Escape would be as easy as that.

Aunt Loris called her downstairs to help in the kitchen and she made plans behind a carefully sustained expression that showed nothing at all. "I'll wait until the doctor's finished looking at Claire," she thought. "I'll wait on the stairs, and when he comes down I'll tell him everything about this house and the temple. And he'll listen and take me out of here."

She grew jittery from waiting for the sound of the doorbell. The nervousness made her stupid and she spilled and dropped things. Her aunt grew more and more terse with her. "I'll be thankful when tomorrow comes and you're off our hands," she said angrily.

The doctor didn't arrive until late afternoon, and Mr Tyrell had to turn on the light in the hall to unlock the front door. Frances watched through the door of the laundry, where she'd been sent to sort out the ironing. The doctor went straight upstairs with Mr Tyrell, and Frances crept after them. Outside Helen's room, where the angle of the stairs made it impossible for two people to pass by each other. That would be the perfect place to hold the doctor's attention, when he came from seeing Claire. And he'd have to stand there and listen until she finished. It wasn't like a telephone, where the person on the other end could hang up on her unlikely story.

She waited just inside Helen's room, her eyes fastened on the closed door of the attic. "You're not to go up there and disturb them," Helen said quickly, looking up from her book.

"I wasn't going to," Frances said. She remembered the times during the past months when Helen had been the only person in that house who had shown anything that resembled friendliness. She wished suddenly that her departure needn't be in such a manner. As soon as she confronted the doctor, the Tyrells' careful, secret way of life would come tumbling down like a card castle. And the pity of it was that they had assembled the cards with as much trust and labour as though they were paving stones.

She could hear the doctor's low voice behind the closed door, murmuring on and on, with nobody interrupting him or asking him questions. "That doctor talks a lot," she said impatiently. "He shouldn't, when Claire's so sick. Sick people don't want to listen to anyone nattering at them."

"Mr Hertes knows what he's about," Helen said. "He cured Rosgrana's migraine headaches once. We usually see him at the temple when we're sick, but Claire's too ill to be moved. That's why he's come to the house instead. He's not a doctor. He's a spiritual healer and a member of the temple council."

Frances kept her eyes on the door of the attic and slowly counted to fifty while she battled away despair. In her mind she saw immense dark clouds creeping across a night sky, blotting out each star from horizon to horizon.

"Father wouldn't allow an ordinary doctor to come inside this house. We don't have anything to do with them. We always see Mr Hertes. Claire's never been as ill as this; none of us ever have. They think it might be caused by your being here; that you've destroyed the harmony, and Claire will start to get better once you've gone."

"That's rubbish!" Frances cried. "Illness isn't caused like that at all! Not the sort Claire's got, coughing and having a fever . . . I didn't have anything to do with it!"

"I tried to tell them so. Claire and Rosgrana kept saying that they couldn't concentrate anymore, with you living in the house, how distracting it was. Father was so worried that all our teaching would be affected. Frances, I'm so sorry that I couldn't do anything to change the way they felt. I tried to . . ."

The attic door opened and Mr Tyrell and the man came down the stairs. Frances shrank back out of sight, alarmed enough to think that she might be whisked out of the house that minute and taken away to live at the temple. There wasn't anything particularly frightening about Mr Hertes. She'd imagined that a member of the temple council would be quite different from anyone else, and show physical evidence of possessing strange and terrible powers. But Mr Hertes wasn't remarkable in any way. He was just a short middle-aged man with receding hair. He'd combed strands across in an effort to minimize the baldness. It was ludicrous to be afraid of anyone so ordinary. Frances tiptoed to the head of the stairs after they passed and looked down.

Mr Tyrell had unlocked the front door and its screen and was helping Mr Hertes on with his coat. Mr Hertes turned to put his arms into the sleeves and noticed Frances. "Ah, the little girl who has been having difficulties," he said. He beckoned her to come down into the hall, and held out his hand for her to shake. Frances took it unwillingly, disliking the way he stared at her. "It's a very great pity that things have turned out in such a disappointing way," he said. "Someone of your age should allow themselves to be guided. You've caused everyone a lot of worry."

Frances looked along the hall at Aunt Loris, hoping for an ally, but her aunt seemed only too eager to agree. "Frances has been a thorough disappointment," she said righteously. "Everyone here has shown her the proper way to do things, and she wouldn't listen. She just wants no part of it. It's very sad, my own niece, and not being able to reach her, or get her to see the truth."

"We thought from the first that she might need more intensive training than you people could give her in this house," Mr Hertes said. "But I'm sure she'll learn quickly during her stay at the temple. She'll eventually become just as much a child of light as Claire or Helen or Rosgrana. What do you think, Frances?"

Frances abruptly tore her hand loose from his. She ducked under his arm through the unlocked door and ran. She wrenched open the gate and fled into the dusk, where the street lamps spilled great bronze pools amongst the shadows. She ran diagonally across the street towards the nearest house with light showing. The softly glowing amber squares of windows promised people, ordinary rational people who would take her in out of the darkness. She sped up a pathway and banged hysterically at the door.

Turning her head, she saw Mr Tyrell and her aunt had come out onto the pavement and were standing under the street lamp. Mr Tyrell was preparing to cross the road, not running in frenzied desperation as she had done. He stood under the street lamp and looked calmly in both directions to check for traffic.

Frances pounded on the door. There were slow footsteps on the other side, and a woman opened it and looked out at her.

"Listen . . . there's a sick girl . . . they won't let me out . . ."

The woman had a rounded dreamy face and slow ways. She took off her glasses and rubbed them on her apron and peered at Frances huddled on her doorstep. "What is it?" she asked. "I can't understand you, dear, what you're saying . . ."

"I want to go back to school and they won't let me," Frances cried, shaken into tears. "I want Kerry . . . They never let me out . . . I never . . ." Her half sentences winged into the darkness like frightened birds.

Mr Tyrell and her aunt had crossed the street. They walked sedately up the pathway of the house and the woman glanced at them over Frances's shoulder.

"Please . . ." sobbed Frances. "I don't want to go back to that place! Can't you . . ."

"What is it you want, love?" the woman asked. Aunt Loris and Mr Tyrell stepped up on the porch, and Mr Tyrell put his arm around Frances and held her tight. "I can't understand anything she's saying, babbling on like that," said the woman. Mr Tyrell smiled at her with immense charm.

"I'm so sorry our little niece disturbed you," he said. "She's mentally handicapped. She's at a special school and becomes confused when she's in a strange house. We're looking after her for the night."

"We left the front door open and she wandered off," Aunt Loris said.

"Poor little Margaret," Mr Tyrell said gently, stroking Frances' hair. "There's no need to cry. We found you again. There's nothing to worry about."

Their soft voices lapped at Frances, drowned her. "Please . . ." she whispered. "Please, they won't let me . . ."

"Sad, isn't it?" said the woman with easy sympathy. "Poor little thing, she could have got hit by a car. Must be a handful for you to mind." She looked at Frances uncertainly, her look a mixture of the embarrassment with which people regard handicapped people in public and a barely concealed thankfulness that she did not have to be personally involved.

45

Mr Tyrell's hand closed around Frances' arm, just above her elbow. The grip was strong enough to pull her away from the door and off the porch. "Silly goose," he said lightly. "Giving your aunt and uncle such a fright, and bothering the neighbours."

The woman stepped out onto her porch and watched Mr Tyrell walk Frances down the path to the gate. "She's very upset, isn't she, poor little soul?" she said to Aunt Loris. "We don't know our own blessings until we realize there are kiddies like that, needing that much care and attention."

"I don't want to go back to that house!" Frances shrieked, hooking her free hand around the gate post and clinging.

"The special school she goes to is lovely and modern," Aunt Loris told the woman. "It's a sort of nursing home, where she boards. She gets into a state when her routine's interrupted. They've got a flu epidemic at that school and they're a bit short-staffed. That's why the matron rang and asked us to have her tonight. She'll settle down. Always does. Thank you for being so understanding about it. I suppose it gave you a turn, her banging on your front door like that. She's a bit spoiled, too, and a right little madam if she doesn't get her own way. But you mustn't let us keep you out in the cold like this any longer."

Mr Tyrell unclamped Frances' hand from the gate post and picked her up easily and carried her across the road. She looked back at the house whose lighted windows had promised sanctuary. Its front door was closing now.

Aunt Loris hurried across to join them and when she was inside the Tyrells' house, Mr Tyrell put Frances down and shut the door. "There's no point crying," he said. "It was very selfish and foolish of you to run off like that, but there's no harm done."

"I'll get out again tonight!" Frances said. "I'll smash the windows and get out and make that woman over there listen to me."

"Can't she go to the temple tonight, Mr Hertes?" Aunt Loris asked tiredly.

"The staff assigned to Frances won't be available until tomorrow morning. Meanwhile, you must take steps to see that she doesn't cause any more potentially dangerous situations for this house. Once she's at the temple, of course, the responsibility will be out of your hands. And quite a responsibility it's going to be. I hadn't realized the extent . . ."

"When I get out of here tonight, I'll tell them all about that temple!" Frances said. "I'll tell the police where it is!"

Mr Hertes stared at her intently.

"I know where your precious temple is!" Frances cried. "I followed Aunt Loris there the day she got married, and I'd know that crummy building anywhere. It's five streets up from a station called Bowan. It looks like a barracks or a prison or something, and I'm not going to live there! You can't shove people in there if they don't want to go, and that's why I'm going to get the police. They'll find all your files and everything . . ."

Her voice, racing after her thoughts, stopped abruptly. She could tell from Mr Hertes's face that a person who knew the whereabouts of the temple was in danger.

"Frances will change, after she's lived at the temple," Helen said urgently. "I know she will. It will be all right, Mr Hertes. Frances will accept the teachings."

"She won't have any choice but to accept them," said Mr Hertes. "Not now."

Robin Klein
*Illustrated by* Tilly Barton

Messages in Bottles

Stories of castaways trapped on desert islands, far from normal shipping lanes, often tell of them placing a rescue plea in a corked bottle and then throwing it into the sea in the hope that ocean currents would carry it to some civilized shore.

Fiction, or fact?

Fact. A surprising number of messages in bottles have turned up, most of them too late to be of any use. For instance:

A bottle was picked up on a Japanese beach in 1864. In it, written on chips of wood, was a story of a treasure hunt gone sadly wrong. Seaman Chunosuke Matsuyama had been hunting for treasure in the Pacific when his ship was caught in a gale. The ship went down and Matsuyama and 44 shipmates were marooned on a lonely coral reef.

Was there time to save them? Alas, no. The castaways had all died of exposure and starvation long, long before. You see, the message had been written in 1714, one hundred and fifty years earlier. What was a strange coincidence was that the bottle was washed up on the very beach Matsuyama had played on as a child.

A story with a happier ending, one with a modern setting and a different twist:

In 1979, while on a Christmas cruise to Hawaii, an American couple, Dorothy and John Peckham, tossed a corked bottle overboard into the Pacific. Inside was an American dollar and a slip of paper carrying their names and address and the request that whoever found the bottle would use the money to post a letter telling the Peckhams how far the bottle had travelled.

Over three years later a reply came — from Thailand! But the writer was not a Thai. Hoa Van Nguyen was Vietnamese, and he and his family had been escaping from Vietnam in a rickety old river boat when he spied the bottle bobbing around in the sea 1400 kilometres off the coast of Thailand. As it happened, Hoa Van Nguyen had been in the South Vietnamese army and had learned English from the American soldiers, so he was able both to understand the message and to write a reply.

Impressed that Hoa Van Nguyen had taken the trouble to write instead of just keeping the dollar (which would have bought a lot of food for a starving family), the Peckhams wrote back for more information and — to cut a long story short — ended up sponsoring the family to come to the United States. So in 1984, thanks to a message in a bottle that travelled almost 13 500 km, a family found a new home.

Name: _Robin Klein_

Born at: _KEMPSEY, N.S.W_

on: _FEBRUARY 28th, 1936_

Started school at: _West Kempsey Primary School_

Favourite subjects: _Reading, Writing_

Liked best: _Reading_

Hated most: _Maths and Sport._

Favourite food when young: _Fruit salad ice blocks_

Favourite food now: _Vegetables_

Jane Eyre

INK

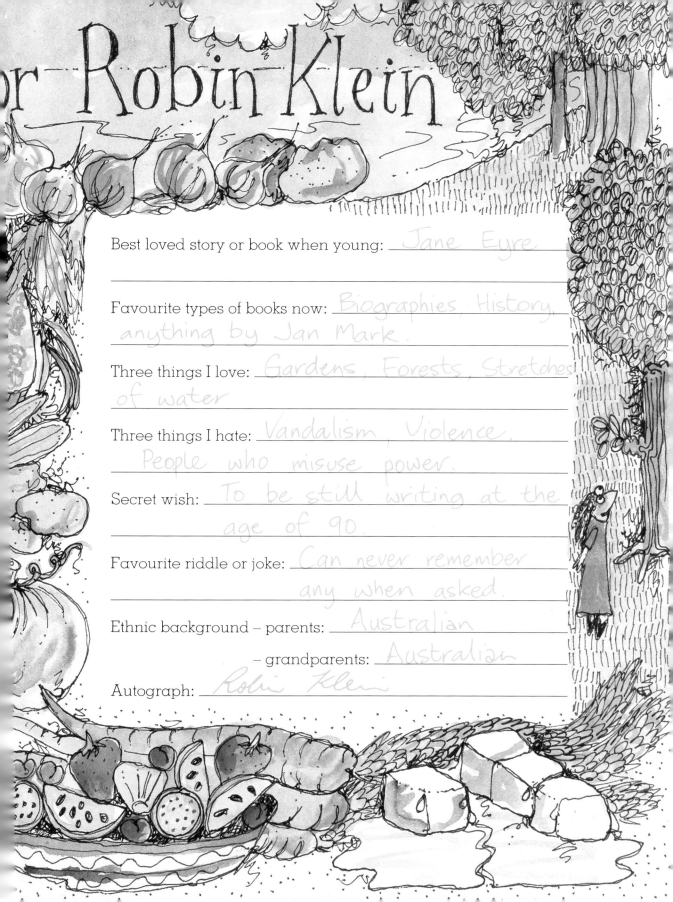

# or Robin Klein

Best loved story or book when young: Jane Eyre

Favourite types of books now: Biographies, History, anything by Jan Mark.

Three things I love: Gardens, Forests, Stretches of water

Three things I hate: Vandalism, Violence, People who misuse power.

Secret wish: To be still writing at the age of 90.

Favourite riddle or joke: Can never remember any when asked.

Ethnic background – parents: Australian

– grandparents: Australian

Autograph: Robin Klein

# JACK AND THE BEANSTALK

Jack's mother said, "We're *stony broke!*
"Go out and find some wealthy bloke
"Who'll buy our cow. Just say she's sound
"And worth at least a hundred pound.
"But don't you dare to let him know
"That she's as old as billy-o."
Jack led the old brown cow away,
And came back later in the day,
And said, "Oh mumsie dear, guess what
"Your clever little boy has got.
"I got, I really don't know how,
"A super trade-in for our cow."
The mother said, "You little creep,
"I'll bet you sold her much too cheap."

When Jack produced one lousy bean,
His startled mother, turning green,
Leaped high up in the air and cried,
"I'm *absolutely stupefied*!
"You crazy boy! D'you really mean
"You sold our Daisy for a bean?"
She snatched the bean. She yelled, "You chump!"
And flung it on the rubbish-dump.
Then summoning up all her power,
She beat the boy for half an hour,
Using (and nothing could be meaner)
The handle of a vacuum-cleaner.
At ten p.m. or thereabout,
The little bean began to sprout.
By morning it had grown so tall
You couldn't see the top at all.
Young Jack cried, "Mum, admit it now!
"It's better than a rotten cow!"
The mother said, "You lunatic!
"Where are the beans that I can pick?
"There's not *one bean*! It's bare as bare!"
"No no!" cried Jack. "You look up there!
"Look very high and you'll behold
"Each single leaf is solid gold!"
By gollikins, the boy was right!
Now, glistening in the morning light,
The mother actually perceives
A mass of lovely golden leaves!

She yells out loud, "My sainted souls!
"I'll sell the Mini, buy a Rolls!
"Don't stand and gape, you little clot!
"Get up there quick and grab the lot!"
Jack was nimble, Jack was keen.
He scrambled up the mighty bean.
Up up he went without a stop,
But just as he was near the top,
A ghastly frightening thing occurred —
Not far above his head he heard
A big deep voice, a rumbling thing
That made the very heavens ring.
It shouted loud, "FEE FI FO FUM
"I SMELL THE BLOOD OF AN
    ENGLISHMAN!"
Jack was frightened, Jack was quick,
And down he climbed in half a tick.

"Oh mum!" he gasped. "Believe you me
"There's something nasty up our tree!
"I saw him, mum! My gizzard froze!
"A Giant with a clever nose!"
"A *clever nose!*" his mother hissed.
"You must be going round the twist!"
"He smelled me out, I swear it, mum!
"He said he *smelled* an Englishman!"
The mother said, "And well he might!
"I've told you every single night
"To take a bath because you smell,
"But would you do it? Would you hell!
"You even make your mother shrink
"Because of your unholy stink!"
Jack answered, "Well, if you're so clean
"Why don't *you* climb the crazy bean."
The mother cried, "By gad, I will!
"There's life within the old dog still!"
She hitched her skirts above her knee
And disappeared right up the tree.

Now would the Giant smell his mum?
Jack listened for the *fee-fo-fum*.
He gazed aloft. He wondered when
The dreaded words would come . . . And then . . .
From somewhere high above the ground
There came a frightful crunching sound
He heard the Giant mutter twice,
"By gosh, that tasted very nice.
"Although" (and this in grumpy tones)
"I wish there weren't so many bones."
"By Christopher!" Jack cried. "By gum!
"The Giant's eaten up my mum!
"He smelled her out! She's in his belly!
"I had a hunch that she was smelly."
Jack stood there gazing longingly
Upon the huge and golden tree.
He murmured softly, "Golly-gosh,
"I guess I'll *have* to take a wash
"If I am going to climb this tree
"Without the Giant smelling me.
"In fact, a bath's my only hope . . ."

He rushed indoors and grabbed the soap
He scrubbed his body everywhere.
He even washed and rinsed his hair.
He did his teeth, he blew his nose
And went out smelling like a rose.
Once more he climbed the mighty bean.
The Giant sat there, gross, obscene,
Muttering through his vicious teeth
(While Jack sat tensely just beneath),
Muttering loud, "FEE FI FO FUM,
"RIGHT NOW I CAN'T SMELL ANYONE."
Jack waited till the Giant slept,
Then out along the boughs he crept
And gathered so such gold, I swear
He was an instant millionaire.
"A bath," he said, "does seem to pay.
"I'm going to have one every day."

Roald Dahl
*Illustrated by Quentin Blake*

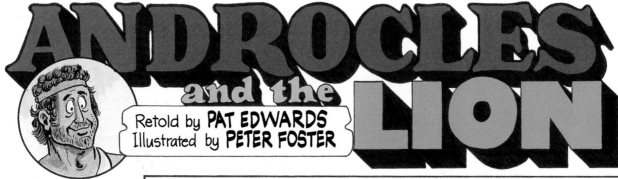

# ANDROCLES and the LION

Retold by **PAT EDWARDS**
Illustrated by **PETER FOSTER**

This tale was told by the Roman author Aulus Gellius who lived around 130-180. A similar story is found in Aesop's Fables, so it's possible the Roman borrowed it from the Greek storyteller. George Bernard Shaw also used it for his play *Androcles and the Lion*, written in 1912.

**A**ndrocles was in trouble. A runaway slave in any Roman province had little future. If he stayed around the town he was sure to be captured and tortured before being put to death as an example to others. If he wandered out into the wild countryside, he would die, either of starvation, or by being attacked and eaten by wild animals. It wasn't much of a choice!

I'll spend the night in this empty cave and decide what to do tomorrow!

But the cave was not empty.

RROAORRR!

Help! I'm a dead man!

But something wonderful happened.

I don't believe it!

The lion is *licking* him!

PRRRRRRRRRRR

What's happening? The lion is *purring!*

Three cheers for the slave who tamed the lion!

He's a miracle worker!

you'll never walk alone

Why, it's my old friend from the desert!

You ol' *smoocher,* you!

PURRR

CHUCK!

CHUCK!

What could the Emperor do but pardon Androcles and make him a free man.

Come, Leo!

It would be nice to think Androcles and the lion lived happily ever after but, alas, the story doesn't tell us that!

**MORAL**

Always take time to do a good deed, even when in a tight corner yourself.

63

# Set the Sun Free

Long, long ago, an ancient Aboriginal tale tells us, the sky was so close to the earth it shut out all light. Dark was the land, dark and cold. So low was the sky, all living things were forced to crawl around in the darkness gathering food with beak, paw and hand, groping to find the way to nest, burrow or cave.

It might still be that way if it hadn't been for the magpies.

"Why can't we raise the sky?" they asked.

"It's too heavy", the others replied.

"Not if we all work together," cried the magpies. But as always happens when there is work to do, no one was ready to help.

"Then we'll do it alone" they said.

Patiently they gathered together the longest sticks they could find and slowly, ever so slowly, they lifted the sky by propping it up so that it no longer hung heavy and low across the land. Animals and birds from all around lifted their heads. Kangaroos stood tall on their hind legs for the first time. Emus and brolgas stretched long-cramped legs. Everyone looked up. And at that moment, while the magpies were struggling to lift the sky even higher, it suddenly split open, setting the sun free to shine over the long-dark land. So magical was the sight of earth's first sunrise, the magpies burst into a joyous carol of welcome and, as they sang, the heavy sky blanket of darkness dissolved into wisps of cloud and drifted away.

And to this day, you'll hear the magpies' happy shout each morning the sun brings light and warmth back to earth.

*An Aboriginal story, re-told and illustrated by Pat Edwards.*

# An Eagle

An Eagle soars UP to the sky,
Flapping his strong, sturdy wings,

Its telescope eyes spotting something on the ground,

As if it has been hit by a war plane,

Screeching

and plunging

towards
its
prey

as if asking for help.

It attacks and swoops and swoops,

Attacks

Until its prey is dead.

Clutching it with sharp claws,

It pecks and eats its prize

And soars back into the skies.

by Lucy Bassett
aged 12

# Prisoner in the Grave

*It is the year 1757. Fifteen year old John Trenchard lives with his aunt in the village of Moonfleet. Once its name was Mohune-fleet, named for the Mohune family who'd been lords of the district and the River Fleet on which it lies. A local tale tells of Blackbeard, one John Mohune, who cheated King Charles I out of a great diamond and then hid it. Now, they say, Blackbeard's ghost constantly hunts for the treasure, and when a villager, Cracky Jones, is found dead in the graveyard, many are certain he'd met the ghost.*

*John knows several of the village men are smugglers. Recently David Black, also 15, was killed by a shot from the Revenue (or customs) men's ship. He also knows that on board that ship was Mr Maskew, a local landowner who'd betrayed the smugglers' plans to the law. Elzevir (David's father), landlord of the Why Not Inn, is very bitter.*

*Not long before this extract starts, John and Ratsey, the sexton, hear a strange rumbling sound under the ground of the church graveyard. The minister, Mr Glenny, explains that the underground grave-rooms (where those of one family were buried) often flooded, making the coffins bump around in the water. On a later visit, John discovers that recent rain has caused the earth to fall away under a gravestone, leaving a hole which leads to the beginning of a sloping passage. He is certain it will lead him to Blackbeard's diamond, so that night . . .*

The moon was bright. I did not take off my clothes, but lay down on my bed — and waited.

After waiting a long time I knew my aunt must be sleeping. I took off my shoes and went quietly down. I found a good candle in my aunt's store-room. Then I went quietly out of the house.

I kept in the shadows as I walked along the street. Everyone was asleep in Moonfleet, and there were no lights in any of the windows except in the Why Not. I went close to the window of the inn and tried to see inside. I could not see in, but I heard a number of voices. What were they all talking about so late at night?

When I reached the graveyard I began to feel afraid. This was the place and time that Blackbeard had loved, and I quite expected to see him spring out from the shadows. But nothing moved. There was no sound but that of my feet moving across the grass. I looked at the hole under the stone, and I stood uncertain whether to go on or back. Then, to my surprise, I saw a boat lying near the shore. It was a strange thing for a boat to be in Moonfleet Bay so late at night. Then I saw a blue light on the boat. I knew that it was a smugglers' boat, and that the seamen were telling someone on shore that they were there ready. I took one last look round and entered the hole.

Holding my candle high up in front of me, I walked down the passage. I was still thinking of the diamond and all the things I would do when I was rich. There were many marks of feet on the ground — more than I had seen before. This made me fear that perhaps someone else had been there before me and found the diamond.

Although this journey seemed a mile long, it was really only twenty yards. At last I came to a stone wall which had once been built across the passage, but now was broken so as to make a door into a room beyond. There I stood, wondering what sort of a place I had come to. Then I suddenly knew that this was the grave of the Mohunes.

I went through the door and found myself in a large room, larger than our school-room, but not so high. It was only about nine feet from the floor to the roof. The floor was of sand. At one end were some steps leading up. All round the sides were the coffins of the Mohunes, each set in a hole in the wall.

But in the middle of the room was something very different. Here lay a great number of boxes and barrels, large and small — smuggled goods!

Here, indeed, was a discovery, for instead of finding Blackbeard's diamond, I had found the Mohunes' grave being used, not as a grave, but as a store-room for smuggled goods!

Now I understand what we had heard on that Sunday afternoon in the graveyard. It was not only the coffins, but these boxes and barrels which were being moved by the water. And Ratsey, the smuggler, had come next day because he feared that the hiding-place might be discovered. I could see the mark where the water had been on the walls within two feet of the roof.

I then began to think of the diamond again and how to get it. I looked closely at the coffins, but most of them had no names on them. I began to think that I would never find anything in this place. I was just turning to go back, when I heard the church bell sounding the hour — twelve. Moonfleet was very proud of its bell and it had a wonderful ringing sound, but it sounded very strange to me in that underground room — one could not tell where the sound began or ended.

Before the sound of the bell had died away I knew that there was some other sound in the air and that someone was coming towards the place. At first I could not tell what this new sound was. Then it came nearer and nearer and I knew that it was the sound of voices talking. They were a long way off at first. I stood, half dead with fear. One minute seemed like a whole hour. Even now, many years after, I can remember how I stood waiting. I was caught like a fox in a hole, caught by smugglers — and I had heard that smugglers had a good way of silencing people who knew too much. I thought of poor Cracky Jones found dead in the graveyard, and how men *said* that he had met Blackbeard in the night.

Then I heard a man jump down into the passage. I took a quick look round to see if there was any way of escape. I could see no way out. There was a man speaking now from the bottom of the hole to others in the graveyard. Suddenly I noticed a great wooden coffin that lay by itself near the top of the wall, six feet up above the ground. Here was a place in which I might hide! I climbed up quickly and lay down between the wall and the coffin. It was so narrow I had to lie on one side. There I lay, while the glimmer of candles threw shadows on the roof as the men came nearer and nearer.

"I can soon fill up the hole," said Ratsey; "and no one will know that it was ever there."

"Be careful," said another, "and do not let anyone see you working there."

More men came in.

"I was in Dorchester three days ago," said a man. "They say there that the smugglers whom they caught last summer will be hanged. Maskew has been there: it was he who wanted to have the men hanged."

"Ah, Maskew! If ever I meet Maskew, I'll kill him!"

"I should like to meet him on a dark night," said another; "I would deal with him!"

"No, you would not!" It was Elzevir's voice speaking. "No, you shall not! No one but I shall deal with Maskew. I remember my son whom he killed. Leave him to me!"

The smell of the lamps, and of the smuggled goods, and the crowd of men made the air so bad that I felt sick. Then I felt a pain in my side caused by lying so long in one place. I was pulling myself round to lie on the other side, when suddenly I heard my own name.

"There is a boy of Trenchard's," said a voice. It was Parmiter speaking; he was a seaman who lived at the north end of the village. "He is always wandering about in the graveyard. I have often seen him sitting on the stone above here looking out to sea. As the sun went down, I looked at the shore from our ship, and there on the stone I saw young Trenchard. I could not see his face, but I knew him by his shape. I fear that he is watching us and then telling Maskew."

"You're right," said Greening of Ringstave, a village near Moonfleet. I knew Greening's slow way of speaking. "When I have been watching Maskew's house, I have often seen this boy walk round the place with a strange look, looking closely at the house."

What Greening said was true, for on summer evening I would walk along the path that led up the hill behind Mr. Maskew's house. I did this for two reasons — it was a beautiful walk which I greatly enjoyed; and I always hoped that I might see Grace, Maskew's daughter. I would sit on an old fence at the end of the garden and watch the house; and sometimes I saw Grace, in a white dress, walking outside in the garden, and sometimes I would pass her window near enough to wave my hand to her. And once, when she was ill, I could not study at school, but sat on the fence the whole day, looking at the house where she lay ill.

So it was true that I had watched the house. But I did not tell anything to Mr. Maskew.

Then Ratsey spoke up for me and said:

"No, no! Trenchard is a good boy. He has told me many times he likes sitting in the graveyard because he can see the sea so well from there; and he loves the sea."

And then to my surprise Elzevir spoke also.

"John Trenchard is a brave boy; I wish he were my son. He is just David's age and he will make a good seaman later on."

These were simple words and yet they pleased me much, for Elzevir spoke as if he meant them. I like Elzevir. I was very sad when I heard that he had lost his son. And, as he spoke, I wanted to jump out and cry "Here I am," but I knew that it would be a foolish thing to do. I lay quiet again.

They had now brought in all the boxes and barrels. They sat down, and Greening began to sing. But Elzevir stopped him.

"Silence, you fool," he said, "you make noise enough to wake the people in the village."

"And if they did wake," said Ratsey, "they would only say it was Blackbeard calling to the Mohunes to help him find his diamond."

But it was clear that Elzevir was the leader. There was silence for a minute. Then one of the men said, "Elzevir is right. Let us go away. It is very late and we have to get back to the ship."

The men went away from the grave of the Mohunes. The light grew dimmer. The foot-steps were more and more distant as they went up the passage, and then I was alone — with the dead in their coffins all round me. Yet for a long time — (it seemed hours) — I could hear the voices far, far away. I knew that some men were standing talking at the end of the passage. Perhaps they were asking how the hole could be filled so that no one might see it. So long as I heard them talking, I dared not come down from my place. I feared that one of them might come back down the passage.

At last I sat up. I decided that I would go home now. I did not want to look for the diamond. I was tired and needed food. So I began to climb down from my place. But to get out of my hiding-place was harder than to get in. I could see by the light of my candle that the coffin by my side was almost turned to dust by age. It was difficult to climb over it, and I dared not put my knee on it.

I do not know how it happened, but just as I was climbing over the coffin, I fell. The candle fell down to the floor. I put out my hand and seized the coffin to save myself falling down also, but my hand went right through the top of the coffin, and I came to the ground in a cloud of dust and broken bits of wood. But all the time I kept in my fingers some hard thing which I had seized in the coffin: I did not know what it was.

I found my candle, and then by its light I looked at the thing in my hand. Mixed with dust there was a little silver box. It had been round the neck of the dead body in the coffin; and that body was the body of Blackbeard. So I had found the diamond! It must be in this little box. At first I could not open it, but at last, working with my fingers at the back of it, I got it open. There was no diamond in it, nor any other jewel, — nothing but a little piece of paper. Perhaps this paper would have a plan on it showing where the diamond might be found. I held it close under the light of my candle. There was writing on it.

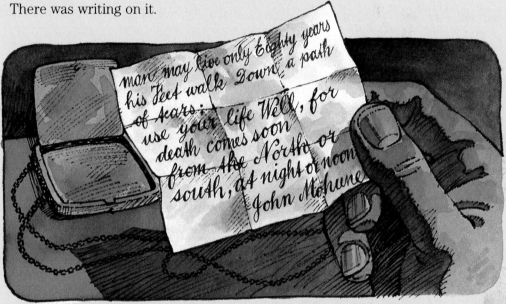

So this was the end of my great hopes. I must go home no richer than when I set out. These foolish lines said nothing of any diamond and did not show where the jewel might be found.

I hung the silver box around my neck. My candle had now burnt so low that I knew I must go home at once. When I came to the end of the passage there was no hole there, for Ratsey had filled it in with earth. At first this did not trouble me, for I thought I could get out easily; but, when I had looked more closely, I did not feel so sure; for they had done good work in filling in the hole and had covered it with old grave-stones.

Then my candle went out and I was in darkness.

I was now in a very bad state, but I was not very much afraid. I sat down to wait for morning, for then (I thought) there would be enough light coming through so that I could see to cut away the earth round the stone. I was very tired. After a little time I fell asleep.

I do not know how long I slept. When I woke, it was still dark. I stood up, but I did not feel so fresh as I should have done after a long sleep. It was dark where I was standing, but, looking up, I could see a glimmer of light coming through the stones above me. And suddenly I knew that I had slept away one whole day, for the light was coming from the setting sun. This was a surprise — a sad surprise for me, for it meant that I must stay another night here.

I began to feel very hungry, not having had anything to eat for twenty-four hours. I also needed something to drink. I tried to move the earth with my fingers, but found that it was hard and dry. After an hour I had done little more than make myself tired and hurt my fingers.

Then I was forced to rest. I sat down on the ground. The last glimmer of light had gone, and the deep blackness of night was upon me again. I lay down and covered my eyes with my arm, so that I might not see how dark it was. Thus I lay for a long time. Then I stood up and shouted, calling to Mr. Glennie and Ratsey and Elzevir to come and save me from this dark place. I tried for many hours to move the earth, but in the end I lay down and slept again.

Many hours passed, and at last I knew by the glimmer of light above that the sun had risen again.

Again I tried to move the earth above me. But a blackness came before my eyes and my head seemed to be turning round and round. I fell —

When I woke I was lying in a nice clean bed. Sunlight was pouring in through the window. Oh, the wonderful sunlight! How I thanked God for the light! At first I though I was in my own bed at my aunt's house and that I had dreamt of the smugglers and of being a prisoner in the darkness. I tried to get up, but fell back on the bed feeling weak and ill. I felt something about my neck, and putting up my hand, I found it was Blackbeard's little silver box. So I knew that it was not a dream, but true.

The door opened and in came Elzevir Block. Then I held up my hands, and cried: "O Elzevir, save me, save me!"

But he, with a kind look on his face, put his hand on my head and said gently: "Lie still, boy, there is none here who will hurt you. Drink this."

He gave me some hot milk. While I drank it, he told me that I was at the Why Not. He would not say more, but told me to get to sleep again, and I should know all later. It was ten days or more before I was well and strong again; and all the time Elzevir watched by me as gently as a woman by her child.

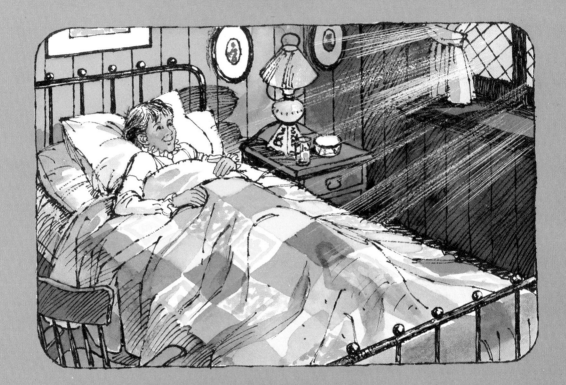

It was Mr. Glennie who had noticed that I was not at school, and he went to ask my aunt if I were ill. My aunt told him that I had run away and she did not know where I had gone. Mr. Glennie then went to Ratsey; but he could tell him nothing. They then thought that I had gone off to sea in a ship.

But the same day Greening came to the Why Not and told a story of having heard loud cries in the graveyard. He said that it must be Blackbeard crying for his diamond.

When he heard this story, Elzevir knew that someone had been caught in the underground passage. He and Ratsey had gone there and found me, lying on the sand, nearly dead.

Elzevir knew that I would not tell anyone about the hidden store-room; but Ratsey, who often came to see me, said: "John, there is only Elzevir and I who know that you have seen our hiding-place; you must tell no one."

As soon as I was stronger, I went up to my aunt's house. She had never come to see me when I was ill, nor asked how I was. She said hard words to me, as she had done to Ratsey when he went to tell her where I was. She told me to go back and stay at the Why Not if I liked it so much. With tears in my eyes, I turned my back on the only home I had ever known.

Written by J. Meade Falkner (simplified by Michael West)
*Illustrated by* Dick Evans

# The Heathen Pirates

*Lucius Bedwyr Marcianus, who lives in the north of Britain, is of Roman ancestry and his family are rich, owning many sheep and cattle. He is called 'lord', even though he is only a young teenager. Long ago, his grandfather had been named king of the area and now his father rules over the community of around ten thousand. Their people are Christian and despise the heathen pirates who sweep down in raids from the far north to pillage and rape the small coastal settlements. The time is around 500 A.D.*

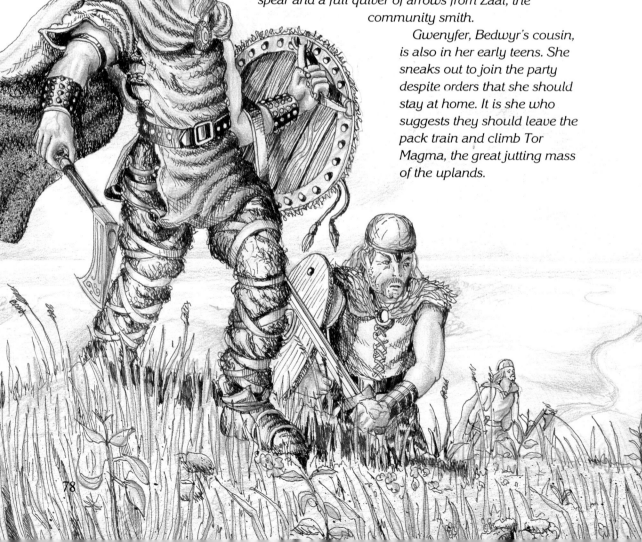

*Bedwyr (as he is called) is delighted when his father gives permission for him to take the kegs of honey ale to the outlying shepherds to help them celebrate the Feast of Saint Alban. With him is Katti, his best friend. Katti, a soldier originally from West Britain, is some years older than Bedwyr. Before leaving they collect a five-foot bore spear and a full quiver of arrows from Zaal, the community smith.*

*Gwenyfer, Bedwyr's cousin, is also in her early teens. She sneaks out to join the party despite orders that she should stay at home. It is she who suggests they should leave the pack train and climb Tor Magma, the great jutting mass of the uplands.*

We ate our midday meal before we went on — it seemed foolish to carry the food to the top, adding to our burden — and then continued on foot and unshod, our footgear slung by their straps round our necks. We climbed noiselessly, perhaps breathing a little harder than usual, but our breathlessness prevented speech. As things turned out, this was perhaps just as well.

There was no track as the slope grew steeper, and we gradually strung out in single file. I was first, being nimbler on my feet than Katti, while my cousin was behind him again, hampered in her climbing by her gown. The last twenty feet or so to the top of the Tor rose steeply, becoming almost a little grass-grown cliff; I had to use my hands to help me climb it, pulling myself up by grasping firmly rooted grass tufts. I reached the top and looked over the edge, and almost cried out at what I saw.

Across the little plateau, not forty feet away, stood a thick-set figure gazing up-river. He wore woollen breeches, cross-gartered, and clumsy shoes of untanned hide, while a leather jerkin clothed his upper body. On his head he wore a leather helmet with an ox-horn set on either side of it. Two other men were clumsily scrambling over the far side of the summit close to him. Although I had never seen one before, I knew well enough what they were: heathen pirates!

All this I saw as I clung there, my feet on an insecure hold of grass-tufts and only the upper part of my head over the ridge. It looked as if the first heathen — the standing one — had himself only just arrived on the crest, and was very naturally looking back the way he had come. Had he been there only a little earlier he would no doubt have come to look in the other direction, and seen us, utterly defenceless, struggling up the slope.

At any moment he might turn, and I would be seen, or one of his struggling followers might see my head outlined against the sky. My heart beat a strong pulse and my throat was dry, but I was not conscious of any fear. Silently I let go of my handhold and slid backwards the way I had come, contriving to gesture Katti to silence as I went past him.

Forty feet below the crest was a clump of bracken, and behind this we lay flat, my cousin between us. We had gestured her to silence also, and she lay between us, puzzled but unafraid. She has always been as good or better than a man in any crisis.

"What's amiss, lord? Did you see something on the top?"

Though Katti kept his voice low, it still sounded over-loud to me.

"I saw three heathen pirates," I said. "One on his feet by the farther edge, and two just breasting the ridge beside him."

"How did you know they were heathen and not some of our own people?"

I described the men's appearance and dress in as few words as I could.

"Did you see anything — a pattern, a device, something coloured — on the front of the leader's jerkin?"

"There was something there, blue-coloured, but I did not see what it was."

Katti nodded. "That would be right — it would be his chief's token, perhaps his own if he were a high man among them." He unslung his bow, and rolled over on his back to string it. When he had done this he rolled forwards again. "Lord, listen well. These men will not be alone, and they must not escape." He looked keenly about. I could tell he was thinking of a plan. "You see that rock over there?"

He pointed past me to a flat tilted slab, one edge level with the ground and the lower part two feet above the surface. I nodded, wondering what was in his mind.

"Cross over to it, then crouch behind it, unslinging your spear. There are loose stones on the ground. Pick a good-sized one, and fling it to the top of the Tor. You can do that, lord?"

I nodded. "And then what?"

"I think they will come over to see where the stone came from. I will get one, perhaps two, with arrows as they look. If I get the horned one, and perhaps one of the others, I think the third will run back the way he came. I can deal with him later. But after you have flung the stone, keep well down. You have no helmet, and they are very good at casting a knife or hatchet."

"And I, Katti?"

"You will stay here, lady. In your green gown you will not be seen in this bracken. Now, lord — go!"

As I crouched and ran for the shelter of the rock to the right, Katti rose and moved to the left, standing up and making no attempt at concealment. He drew three arrows from the quiver, sticking two loosely into the turf in front of him and setting the third on the bowstring. I gained the rock, unslung the spear, and took up a large stone.

My first cast was a failure — I had taken too large a stone, and tried to fling it while kneeling. I took another, stood up, and contrived to lob it over the crest. Then I dropped back behind my rock, but could not resist looking round the edge of it to see what was going to happen.

The results were almost immediate. The horned man strode almost to the edge — and Katti's first arrow took him through the neck from side to side. He fell forward, sliding head-foremost down the steep slope, kicking and gurgling. Twenty feet down his head butted into a rock, and he reared uppermost, almost standing on his head. There was a sharp cracking noise, and he fell back, his limbs twitching. Later we found his neck was broken, although Katti's arrow alone would have killed him.

Not seeing the arrow, his two companions probably thought the edge had crumbled under him, and they sprang back so that I could only see them from the waist up. These seemed to be of a meaner sort than the horned man; their helmets had no ox-horns and their clothing bore no ornament. They were short and thick-set, wearing no beard, with long drooping moustaches. In appearance they were both repulsive and barbarous.

They did not see Katti until he called, a wordless cry, blood-curdling and fierce. As they turned, Katti's second arrow took one of the men in the left eye. He screamed, and plucked at it, trying to draw it out. This was a useless thing to do, had he but known it. Zaal's hunting arrows were so well barbed that they had either to be cut out, or driven right through. While he was riving at it, Katti's third arrow took him through the throat, front to back, pinning his arm to his neck. He dropped, and the screaming stopped.

While Katti plucked a fourth arrow from the quiver at his back, the third man did an unexpected thing. He could not have seen me, but he sprang over the edge of the Tor and came down the slope in giant strides straight at my rock, at the same time plucking a hatchet from his girdle to throw at Katti. His intention was obvious, and even if he missed his throw, he would be a difficult mark to hit going at speed down the hillside.

I do not think he even saw me, at least until it was too late to change his direction. The spearbutt was well bedded down, and I had a firm grip. At the last moment he may have seen the spear head and tried to leap aside, but it was too late — it took him where I intended, in the upper belly, just below the rib-cage. The long blade sank into his body right up to the cross-guard, and the impetus of his weight sank the spearbutt deep into the turf. He fell on top of me, pinning me down behind the rock, the hatchet flying from his dead hand as he fell.

He stank vilely, of unwashed body and foul woollen clothing. I lay beneath him, his body twitching and stirring on top of me, but only for a very short time. Then the body — for he was dead enough, the spearhead had broken his back — was heaved to one side, and Katti helped me to my feet. I leaned against the rock, gasping for breath.

"You are not hurt, lord?"

I nodded, not having breath to speak. Katti put his foot against the belly of my victim and dragged out the spear. The barbs below the head made a tearing sound as he cleared them. I looked at the bloody corpse, and laughed in a silly fashion, until Katti silenced me with a gesture.

"Your first heathen, lord — you have slain at an earlier age than I did. No one could say that you are not well-blooded, either."

There was a great patch of wet blood on the front of my tunic — the dead man's blood. I touched it, fascinated — the slimy feel of it on the well-woven wool of the tunic was horrible. I felt suddenly sick.

"Steady, lord. Put your head down between your knees — that's the way. There were but the three of them, and it's all over for the time being. Sit quiet for awhile."

Presently the blood flowed into my head again, my sight cleared, and I felt better. Katti took handfuls of bracken leaves and rubbed much of the blood from my tunic. Then we went over to where Gwenyfer still hid in the bracken. She cried out when she saw my bloody tunic.

"You are hurt, cousin!"

"Not I. This is heathen blood. I took the third one in the belly with the boar-spear, and he fell on me. That is all." I controlled my voice with an effort, finding I had a tendency to speak over-loudly.

"Oh, horrible!" she said. Then: "I have never seen a heathen. What are they like?"

"No fit sight for you, lady," said Katti. "And as for seeing them, that can wait. We must try to find out where they are from, and what their numbers are. Be good enough to stay here, lady, until we come back."

"But but — the heathen — " she said, indicating the two tumbled corpses.

"Have no fear of them, lady — their teeth are drawn, they cannot bite you. Bide quietly here while the Lord Bedwyr and I spy out the land."

Without a word she seated herself with her back to the dead heathens, took a little comb from the pouch at her girdle and began to re-dress her hair. Then we walked over to the dead heathen leader and Katti cut his arrow free and cleaned the head carefully in a patch of soft turf, telling me to do the same with the ruddied spear-head.

"It is not that I care about my next foeman, lord," he said, "but I was taught this way, and there is good sense in it. Rotting blood or flesh breeds a strong poison, and a scratch from a dirty weapon brings such a death as I would not want the worst heathen to suffer. These must be scalded in a cauldron when we get back to Turris Alba, but until then clean turf is better than nothing."

George Finkel
*Illustrated by Peter Schmidli*

# WHO'S A-MAZE-D?

Or rather, what's a maze, and how do you make one? The dictionary description is "a complex network of paths or passages, especially one with high hedges in a garden, designed to puzzle those walking through it". And it suggests you look up *labyrinth*, which is described as "a maze-like network of tunnels, chambers or paths . . ."

Remember how Theseus had to go into the labyrinth or maze to slay the Minotaur, and how later Daedalus and his son, Icarus, were imprisoned in it? Modern mystery writers still like to trap the hero or heroine inside a maze and there are lots of children's puzzles that involve trying to get in or out of a maze-like design.

Who first thought of all this? Who can say! What is amazing (and yes, the two words do come from the same root) is that the most common simple maze design has been found all over the world — in England, Finland, India, Peru, North America and many Mediterranean countries. Earliest record of it was found on an Italian vase, 2 500 years old.

Here's what it looks like

And here's the way to draw it

| 1 | 2 | 3 | 4 | 5 |
|---|---|---|---|---|

  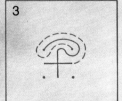  

Okay? Now you're all set to go off and create some amazing maze games that will simply amaze your friends!

# · CAPTIVE ·

*Quen's homeland has been invaded by an alien race — the ugly, squat, grey Mollags who have superhuman strength. Journeys between the ten villages that fringe the holy forest of Thual have been forbidden by these new rulers and many in the land have been enslaved.*

*But now Quen has been sent by his mother into the forest to find the Wise Ones, the Keepers of the Great Eye, in the hope they can help throw off the oppressors. Deep in the forest he meets a strange man named Namu who has a mysterious communication with animals. When Quen leaves Namu's shelter, a small fox appears to lead him on his way. After a time Quen grows careless and ignores the fox's guidance only to be caught in a large rope net — a Mollag trap. When a Mollag releases him, he tries to make a run for it, but a heavy blow from a wooden club breaks his arm.*

*As Quen fights off unconsciousness, the only glimmer of hope remaining is that the Mollag's rough search has not discovered his knife.*

DESPITE his broken arm and the obvious pain he was in, Quen was not allowed to rest throughout the remainder of that day. The squat square-bodied Mollag lumbered along behind, prodding him between the shoulder blades with his club whenever Quen slackened his pace. Nursing his injured left arm with his other hand, he stumbled down the gloomy tree-covered trail for mile after mile, continually on the lookout for a chance of breaking free of his captor. But what little hope he still had seemed to vanish altogether when, late in the afternoon, they were joined by another Mollag — a huge evil-smelling figure dressed in greasy leather and scarred greenish-bronze plates. He let out a great roar when he saw Quen and cuffed him on the side of the head, knocking him down; but immediately the other Mollag restrained him, rasping out something in his own tongue, and together all three moved off once again, Quen travelling between them, half-choked by the corpse-like smell of the two grey-skinned soldiers.

The Mollag themselves would not normally have stopped to rest, but soon after nightfall Quen was so obviously tired out that it was a question of either carrying him or allowing him to sleep.

They debated the matter in their clipped metallic speech and finally threw him down beneath a tree and lit a small fire of leaves and twigs. Each of them carried a light pack on his back, and from these they took stringy pieces of raw sour-smelling meat which they singed on the fire and wolfed down. One of them tossed a piece to Quen, but he kicked it away with his foot, refusing even to touch it.

"As hunger grows inside you," the Mollag said, "you will learn to act differently. In a day or two you will beg us for the scraps that fall from our fingers."

"A day or two?" Quen asked sharply. "Where are you taking me then?"

"To where you came from: back to the ten villages."

The thought of retracing all those miles only to face his parents with nothing achieved was almost more than he could bear at that moment, tired and dispirited as he was.

"But why there?" he cried. "Why not ask me what you want now? Do what you have to do here and be done with it."

"Be silent!" the Mollag ordered. "It is not for us to question you. You are to be taken before Ungeth. That is his command."

Quen had heard vague rumours of there being a Mollag leader; yet nobody had been sure that such a figure actually existed.

"Who is Ungeth?" he asked. "Is he your king?"

"King!" the Mollag said disdainfully. "He cannot be described by such stupid words. He is Ungeth, the supreme one. Now be quiet and sleep. There will be no more talk until we bring you before him."

The Mollag came over to where Quen lay and tied his hands and legs together with leather thongs. Quen did not resist. For some reason which he did not fully understand, the knowledge that the Mollag were subject to a supreme leader cheered him slightly. Somehow it gave him the feeling that he was not up against a whole army, but simply one figure — Ungeth. His dying hopes suddenly flickered alive again: perhaps, after all, there was a weakness at the very heart of the vast Mollag strength.

Although Quen was tired, he struggled to stay awake. Now, more than ever, he felt the need to regain his freedom. Through half-closed eyes he watched the two Mollag muttering beside the fire. Beyond them the forest formed a single black curtain which the tiny fire could not penetrate. Quen was gazing longingly at the promised safety of this darkness when abruptly his attention was caught by a flash of moving light. He blinked to bring himself fully awake and found himself staring at a pair of watchful eyes.

Almost at the same instant the Mollag also noticed the eyes and leaped to their feet; but before they could so much as draw their clubs, a terrible chorus of howls broke out and more than a dozen pairs of eyes appeared in the darkness all around them. Like the Mollag, Quen recognized those howls immediately: they were the cries of a wolf pack which was only yards away, preparing to attack. Quen's first reaction was one of fear. But as the Mollag scrabbled in the fire, searching for brands large enough to fling into the darkness, he realized how foolish he was being. Here, at last, was the opportunity he had hardly dared to hope for.

Ignoring the pain in his broken arm, he arched his back and reached down to his boot, to where the knife was hidden. With the bone handle grasped firmly in his good hand, he sliced through the leather thongs binding his feet. Then, while the Mollag were busy trying to scare off the wolf pack, he rolled over onto his knees and stumbled to his feet.

He had no idea what awaited him beyond the narrow ring of light. It could be a swift death from the savage jaws of the wolves. Yet at that moment even such a possibility seemed preferable to being held and ultimately tortured by the Mollag. And drawing a deep breath, he stepped into darkness.

Directly ahead of him two pairs of eyes glinted threateningly. But instead of coming closer, they narrowed and faded into the darkness on either side. He paused, giving himself a chance to grow used to the sudden darkness; and as he did so, something brushed against his leg. Reaching down with his still-bound hands, he touched a soft furry coat, and just for an instant he thought a wolf had sidled up to him; but then he caught the unmistakable musky smell of fox, and all at once he understood exactly what was happening. This was not really an attack at all, but more a kind of rescue. Somewhere in the forest Namu still protected him. And without any further hesitation he ran off between the trees.

Gradually the shouts of the Mollag and the howling of the wolves faded behind him. The fox had led him directly to a broad path, open to the sky; and now, by the faint light of the stars, he mustered the last of his strength, determined to put as great a distance between himself and the Mollag as possible. He knew they could not follow him at night and that provided he kept moving he could gain six or more hours on them before dawn. Then there would be time to rest. Meanwhile, his immediate task was to reach water and cover his tracks.

As on a previous occasion, the fox seemed to sense his needs, and before the night was half over it had led him to a shallow rocky stream. Here, he stopped for the first time to free his hands. Squatting down, he took the knife between his teeth and sawed through the leather thong. His wrists and fingers were stiff and numb from being bound so long, and it was while he sat, chafing his uninjured hand against his thigh to bring back the circulation, that he realized the full extent of his weariness. Fearful that he might either lose the will to go on or simply sink into an exhausted sleep, he clambered up and splashed off down the rocky bed of the stream.

During the last two hours of darkness, he was forced to slow down. Yet when the sky finally began to lighten he was still moving, though only at a slow unsteady walk. By then he was in desperate need of rest. He had had no sleep for twenty-four hours, and his broken arm jolted him with pain at every step. In addition, a light rain had begun to fall — not enough to cover his tracks, but sufficient to soak him through. Normally, that would not have affected him; but in his exhausted state he was soon chilled to the bone.

In the full light of the new day he looked a sorry sight. With his hair plastered to his forehead, his face pale and drawn, his eyes hollow with fatigue, and his damaged arm swollen and hanging uselessly at his side, he staggered to a halt just where the path divided into two. The fox was already scurrying off, urging him on, but he could go no further and he looked around, searching for a hollow log or tree — any place that was dry and warm, where he could curl up and rest.

The forest, however, had never appeared more unfriendly and forbidding. From a grey overcast sky the rain fell steadily, dripping from the leaves and bushes, streaking the trunks of trees with damp. It seemed impossible to imagine that the sun ever shone in such a dank gloomy place, and the task of finding a dry refuge seemed hopeless. With his teeth chattering uncontrollably, Quen gave up his search almost before

it was begun. Staggering into the partial shelter of a large elm tree, he was about to sink down onto the open ground when he heard the fox give its soft warning bark and he turned to see it scurrying back towards him.

There was now no question of outrunning his pursuers; he had reached a stage where he lacked not only the energy, but also the will to go on. And creeping between the bushes, he climbed over a rotting, fallen log and lay down in the thick wet grass. The fox, after hesitating for a moment, followed him; and together they peered down the narrow track to where it bent away out of sight.

They didn't have long to wait. Through the mist of rain which seemed to hang in the air, Quen saw a flicker of movement and then two figures emerged into full view. To his relief they were not the Mollag. Instead, a man and a woman came walking down the path: both of them tall, with long pale faces, and dressed in full-length white robes and broad-brimmed white hats. Their hair too was long and had been drawn around their faces and tied under the chin. In the case of the man, hair and beard mingled together and covered most of his chest, reaching almost to his waist.

Both man and woman walked slowly, their bright observant eyes continually probing the forest. So as not to be seen, Quen ducked completely out of sight. Nonetheless, as they drew close to where he lay, they became steadily more suspicious, their eyes flashing uneasily from side to side. Finally, when they were directly opposite the fallen log, they stopped altogether.

"It is no use hiding," the woman said. "Come out and show yourself."

At the sound of the low commanding voice, the fox leaped over the log and ran past the two figures as though trying to attract their attention; but they showed no interest in the small animal.

"I know you can hear me," the woman said. "I command you, in the sacred name of Thual, to show yourself."

Quen had no desire to be taken again; common sense told him to remain out of sight and to try to creep further away. Yet somehow that was impossible. An invisible force seemed to envelop him, and almost against his will he found himself slowly rising to his feet and turning to face the fierce shining eyes of these tall unknown figures. As though from a great distance, he heard the man say:

"It is the boy, the one we have been searching for."

And the woman's reply:

"He will have to answer for his presence here."

**Victor Kelleher** *Illustrated by* **Azoo Design**

92

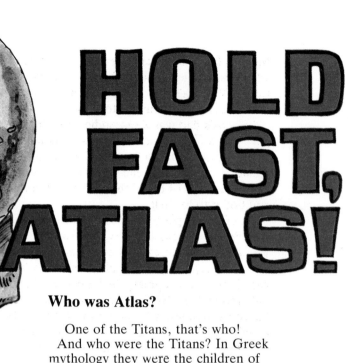

# HOLD FAST, ATLAS!

### Who was Atlas?

One of the Titans, that's who! And who were the Titans? In Greek mythology they were the children of Uranus who was Heaven and Gaea who was Earth. That made them the first gods. Cronus the youngest of the six boy children, overthrew Uranus and ruled over heaven and earth with Rhea his sister and wife. During this time (which became known as the Golden Age), Cronus and Rhea had six children, all but one of whom Cronus swallowed at birth. (Nasty lot, these gods!)

Why did he do it? It seems he had been warned that one of his children would seize the throne from him. However, Rhea saved the youngest, whom she named Zeus, and hid him away on the island of Crete. When Zeus had grown up he rescued his brothers and sisters by forcing Cronus to disgorge them. (Get's worse, doesn't it!) Then, with help from two of his brothers, Pluto and Poseidon, Zeus began a rebellion. There was a mighty battle, but Zeus and his allies won and the Titans were cast into the Underworld—in a deep dark chasm of Hades. All except Atlas, that is. He was condemned to bear the weight of the heavens on his shoulders forever.

Some time later, along comes Perseus (one of the seven great Greek heroes). He's on his way home with the head of Medusa, which he'd promised to fling at the feet of Polydectes, a nasty piece of work who was pestering Perseus's Mum to marry him.

94

Medusa had once been a beautiful maiden, especially famous for her glorious hair, but when she'd fallen foul of Athena, goddess of wisdom, the touchy goddess had promptly turned Medusa's hair into live serpents and made her face so terrible that all who looked at her were turned to stone.

Perseus's dad was Zeus, so he had a bit of pull. Before he set out on his task, Athena gave him a round shield of polished metal and told him to use it as a mirror. Keeping his eyes only on the reflection of Medusa, he was thus able to sneak up on the fearsome creature and cut her head off while she lay sleeping. (The winged horse, Pegasus, rose from the drops of blood that fell from the headless body.) Then he stuffed it in a bag and tied it to his belt.

As often happened in these tales, Perseus got lost on the way home. One night while wearily flying along in the winged sandals he'd been lent by Hermes, he saw that he was above the garden of the Hesperides and decided to pop in and ask if he could stay the night. Now the Hesperides were Atlas's three daughters and it was their job to guard the golden apples which grew on Hera's tree. (Hera knew her husband, Zeus, only too well and she'd transplanted the tree to this lonely place to stop him helping himself and handing them out to whichever fair maiden caught his eye.) Atlas had built a high wall about the garden, so Perseus dropped down and hammered on the gate.

"Mighty Atlas," he yelled, peering up to where the Titan towered far above him.

"Will you let me stay the night?"

"Who are you, bold youth?" roared a voice like thunder.

"Perseus," our hero cried and then, not being above a bit of name-dropping, he added, "and I'm son of Zeus, father of all the gods."

Atlas didn't like the sound of this. He immediately suspected Perseus was here to steal the golden apples and when the brash youth refused to take no for an answer, Atlas bent down and picked him up, ready to toss him into the sea. Angrily, Perseus pulled the head of Medusa from the bag and dangled it in front of the Titan. There was a terrible groaning . . . and Atlas turned to stone.

Legend believes he formed the Atlas mountains in North Africa. The ancient people of Greece and Africa believed the sky rested on the top of these mountains, so it seemed logical that they should once have been the Titan, trapped forever in this role.

## Why should we know about him?

For the very good reason that we all use an atlas at some time or other, so it's interesting to know the derivation of the name. It seems that a drawing of Atlas with the world on his back was put on the title page by Rumold Mercator when he first published his father's maps in 1595. No doubt people began referring to it as 'the book of Atlas' and in time all collections of maps became known simply as atlases.

The name is often used as a trade name by firms or manufacturers (people think of strength when they hear it) and it was chosen for the US intercontinental ballistic missile also used in launching spacecraft.

# A BANQUET IN A CELLAR

*Christine Arnothy was only 15 when she lived through the seige of Budapest in Hungary. She describes how she and her family, along with the other tenants of the bombed-out apartment building in which they'd all been living, huddled in the cold, dark cellar listening in fear as the battle raged above their heads. At first everyone had expected it to be short and sharp, but by the fifth day it became obvious that the Germans had decided to defend the city against the Russians. It is hard living in such close proximity to strangers, and tensions grow as food gets short. An added danger is the mobile AA gun parked outside their building, as it draws extra enemy fire.*

*In the cellar with Christine and her parents are: the janitor, and his wife; Ilus and her six months old baby; a medical student whom everyone calls 'Doctor' and his aunt who is a banker's widow and is a nosey parker, always interfering; 'the colonel's lady' (wife of an army colonel), who felt the fact that she'd been an air raid warden gave her the right to boss everyone around; the district attorney (who had pneumonia) and his wife; and Mr Radnai, a gentle Jew who lived under cover of false papers.*

*After a week, people suddenly begin turning their hatred of the enemy against the others in the cellar. They circle around each other like angry dogs, each watching for the right moment to tear the other to pieces . . .*

It was during one of these deadly evenings that Pista appeared. He came whistling down the steps and, pushing open the door to the main shelter, said simply, with a broad smile: "Good evening! . . . I wish you good evening . . ."

He wore the uniform of the Hungarian infantry. A knapsack hung from his shoulder, and his smile was as radiant as if the sun had suddenly lit up our darkness. We formed a circle around him, looking at him as if he had come from another planet. We wanted to touch him to assure ourselves that this was a real human being and not an invention of our tortured imaginations.

He threw his tommy gun on the floor and declared, "Tonight, I'll sleep here. Do you accept me?"

"Who are you?" asked a voice.

"Istvan Nagy. From Pusztaberény, in the county of Somogy." This introduction sealed our friendship and from then on Pista was one of us. We besieged him with questions: Where were the Russians? How much longer would we have to stay in the cellar? He knew no more than we did. We asked him to which army corps he belonged. "To none that I know of," he replied calmly. "I move around here and there. Now I'll stay here for a while."

He sat down on a stool, took some bread and bacon from his knapsack, and asked how many of us there were.

"Twelve," answered the banker's widow.

Pista divided his bread and bacon into twelve parts so that everyone could have a bite. We watched him, grateful and amazed. The food melted in our empty mouths like a piously whispered prayer of thanksgiving. Pista had miraculously relaxed the tense atmosphere. But suddenly the district attorney's voice came from a corner of the cellar. "Deserter!" he gasped from lungs burning with fever. "Can't you see he's a deserter? At a time like this, he ought to be fighting somewhere — if necessary, shedding his blood . . ."

"What's the matter with the old man?" Pista asked. "Pneumonia" replied the doctor laconically, as if this were a consultation. "I'll try to scrounge a bit of sulfa for him tomorrow," promised Pista. "There's still some in a drugstore in the Boulevard Margit. I've gotten it already for several sick people. But right now, I'm going to sleep. I'm tired."

"Are you really going to bring him some medicine?" asked the district attorney's wife, clutching his arm. "Sulfa — that might still save him . . .

Here, take my mattress to stretch out on."

Pista shook his head.

"That's not necessary. The rug's all right for me. Tomorrow I'll bring the medicine and some flour. There's still lots of flour in a store in Express Street, with that you'll have plenty of food."

That night, toward eleven o'clock, a heavy bomber went all out for us. The ground shook and reverberated under our feet. I buried my head in my pillow. But, suddenly, a strange calm came over me.

"Dear God," I whispered, "Thy will be done . . ."

Pista left at dawn, and while he was away we talked of no one else. The wife of the district attorney anxiously watched for his return because of the medicine; others thrilled at the thought of the flour. Of them all, our family was the worst off for food — just because we had shown too much foresight. By a lucky chance, my parents had been able to rent three rooms in a villa in the Hüvösvölgy, protected by the Swedish flag. From the very beginning of December we had taken all our valuables there as well as quantities of foodstuffs — whole sacks of flour, jars of cooking fat, meat, sugar, coffee, and beverages of all kinds.

We had counted on waiting out the arrival of the Russians at the villa. But they had taken the area before we got there, and we had to give up all hope of reaching our refuge. In the fall, my father had lent the villa to some friends from Transylvania who had a large family. He had told himself that a small space would be big enough to house a large number of people of good will. The result was that they now had all the food they needed, while we were fasting in our cellar. But nothing could be done about it and, if Pista really did bring us flour, our worries would be over. For we needed bread more than anything . . .

In the happy expectation of more flour, even the couple who kept a restaurant on the ground floor of the building had joined us. Up to then, these two had kept away, fearing that the tenants might ask for food. They were unwilling to part with it for money and did not yet dare to demand gold in exchange. But now the restaurant keeper's wife was all honey and offered to cook a goulash for lunch. She was even ready to sacrifice a few cans of meat still in her possession. Everyone was to have some of the stew on the strict condition that she got a third of the flour Pista brought back. We all accepted enthusiastically and she returned to her stove. The hours crept by with exasperating slowness, punctuated only by the jerky rhythm of the bombs.

Toward noon, the cellar assumed a holiday atmosphere. Hearts swelled with joy at the prospect of a good meal. We put a few tables together and covered them with a white cloth; then everyone brought his plate. We waited. Even the district attorney felt better and claimed his share of the goulash. His wife gave the doctor a questioning look: The young man shrugged his shoulders. Nothing could make him any worse . . . let him go ahead and eat.

We were all there, sitting around the table as if for a banquet. At last the restaurant-keeping couple appeared, bearing a large casserole.

They went all around the table and ladled a big helping of stewed meat onto each plate. We giggled with pleasure. Our doctor bedaubed his face with grease up to the ears, and the banker's widow bent close to her plate as if to drink her goulash instead of eating it. Who thought of death then or of the martyred town crumbling to dust over our heads?

Like so many unchained beasts, we flung ourselves on the pieces of meat; then we leaned back comfortably, staring into space, silently savoring the delight of being replete at last. This meal was memorable for every single one of us. The tenants arranged with the restaurant keeper that, from now on, they would take turns making bread in his oven.

About four o'clock in the afternoon, the house was hit by two bombs. Tiles and pieces of roof were flung down into the courtyard. Either our apartment must have been hit or else the district attorney's. It was the front of the building, overlooking the Danube, that had been damaged.

On the twenty-fourth of December in a vain attempt to get to the Hüvösvölgy we had left home so hurriedly that I had left the book I was reading upstairs. It was Balzac's *Peau de Chagrin*. In my mind, I often relived the story I had begun and which I should have liked to finish, but I did not have the courage to go up to the apartment again. The idea of climbing the stairs to the second floor filled me with as much terror as the sight of builders moving about on a narrow plank five floors above the street. In the interval between the two direct hits on the house, I thought of my book, thinking that, even if it were still intact, I should never know how the novel ended because we would — all of us — die here in this cellar.

Sitting on the edge of my bed, I felt my eyes fill with tears at the thought of death. It was not self pity, but an inexplicable sense of loss. Fantastic dreams tormented me at night, and strange adventures, projected in the darkness as on a screen, unrolled before my eyes. I saw myself walking under palm trees on the arm of a young man who never turned his face toward me. I was travelling in an express train and heard the little bell rung by the waiter in the dining car. I went to the theatre and saw the actors speaking words whose sound never reached me. Waking up was always torture: reality, the horrible cellar, the smelly candle and the hollow-eyed shapes wandering about in the half-light. How I longed to take refuge again in the land of dreams! But today's good meal had put me in a better mood, as if the blood flowed faster and warmer in my veins because my hunger was satisfied. And, from now on, there would be bread, lots of good bread.

When he returned toward evening, covered with snow, Pista looked just like Santa Claus. Instead of his knapsack, he had a very heavy sack which he pushed along before him, panting with the effort.

"Weren't you afraid to come such a long way with that big load?" asked Ilus.

Pista smiled.

"I thought the sack would be a protection if a bomb hit me."

The banker's widow sighed.

"At last a fearless man! Just like my poor Albert . . . Is it pastry flour, my friend, or just ordinary bread flour?"

'One third belongs to me," the restaurant keeper's wife broke in. "I've got a right to it, I've fed everybody here, filled all their bellies."

Pista gave her a searching look. Then he took a little oblong box out of his pocket and handed it to the district attorney's wife.

"Here's the sulfa."

The woman began to cry as she thanked him.

We surrounded Pista and all stared at the sack of flour as if hypnotized. A sack of life! Pista ordered each of us to bring some receptacle so that he could distribute it fairly.

"The one with the least food may bring the largest container," he called to us.

"You see how fair he is?" I whispered to my mother.

In my eyes, Pista had become a dazzling hero. He was like the Count of Monte Cristo.

The time had come. Pista untied the sack and filled our casserole ahead of the others. A light film of white dust covered the black cement floor. My mother took the casserole and tasted a pinch of flour. Her face took on a different expression.

"It's only plaster," she murmured. "It's only plaster, not flour at all."

She had spoken these words under her breath but everyone heard. The cellar was transformed into an overturned wasps' nest. Using their elbows, everyone pushed to have a taste, and the restaurant keeper's wife screamed: "You gang of cheats! I gave you food because I was expecting flour and now he's brought plaster and I've fed the lot of you . . ."

Her large face flushed deeper and deeper. Her husband tried vainly to calm her. The woman went toward the door. When she turned to face us, one hand on the latch, I was afraid she had had a stroke, her features were so distorted. But it was only the meanness of her soul that was making her go to pieces before our eyes, while bitter words spurted from her lips.

"The goulash you ate was horse meat, not beef . . . In Duck Street, there's a dead horse . . . We cut up its carcass for your meal. Enjoy yourselves now with all that carrion in your bellies . . ."

She slammed the iron door behind her. Sick at her stomach, Ilus leaned against the wall . . . For a few minutes, one heard nothing but her efforts not to vomit. In my own stomach, the meal lay as heavy as a stone. At that moment it seemed that nothing worse could happen to us.

"I assure you all this is only silly prejudice," Mr. Radnai suddenly exclaimed from the dark corner that hid him. "Horse meat is no worse than pork or beef — it's just that we aren't used to it. There's no point getting so worked up over it."

My father took up the argument, developing it as if he were in his classroom giving a lecture on Horace.

"Was it not also an erroneous idea to believe that there would be no fighting in the city and that the war would thus spare the civilian population? Now that the war has invaded our streets, everyone is a soldier, even the sick, the babies, the women, and the old men. So we ought not to get into a panic on the subject of the goulash . . . we may well meet other ordeals which will demand every ounce of our strength."

"The restaurant man's wife is a witch all the same . . ." said the doctor, ending the debate.

No one contradicted him.

We emptied the disappointing contents of our casserole into the big sack. Suddenly I was seized with such a violent desire to crunch a loaf of good white bread, all hot from the oven, that I felt faint. I returned to our corner and, lying down on the bed, waited for sleep. The ground shook under our feet; machine gun bullets hammered the walls with a hard, dry rattle like a shower of hail. My imagination had almost carried me to the promenade under the palm trees when a sentence reached me through the mists of slumber. It was the voice of my father speaking to my mother: "Pista says they've brought a munitions train along the bank of the Danube, by using the rails of the number 9 streetcar. The last car in the train is opposite our house. We may be blown up at any moment . . ."

Christine Arnothy
*Illustrated by* Rachel Legge

*Christine left Hungary four years later in 1948. She lived in Belgium, working in a bookshop while she wrote her story from the diaries she had kept while trapped in the cellar. She titled her book* I Am Fifteen — and I Don't Want to Die. *It won the Prix de Verites (French prize for non-fiction) the year it was published.*

# The Channel Islands

On a really fine day in Guernsey you can see all the other islands and the coast of France – but not England!

GUERNSEY

Although the Channel Islands are part of the United Kingdom, they govern themselves and make their own laws. Unlike the rest of Britain, they are not part of the Common Market.

The holiday trade is an important source of income for the islands. There are beautiful beaches, magnificent views and water sports galore!

Guernsey and Jersey cows are famous all over the world!

The warmer temperatures of the Channel Islands make them very suitable for growing flowers and fruits which are exported to England and France.

JERSEY

Alderney is famous for its week of summer festivities including processions, bonfires and torchlight celebrations.

ALDERNEY

Sark has no cars at all, but visitors can see the island in a horse and carriage! Local people use bikes, tractors or their feet!

SARK

Guernseys and Jerseys are sweaters that the fishermen used to wear.

During the Second World War, the Channel Islands were captured and occupied by the Germans.

Jersey has an annual Battle of Flowers which is a procession of huge floats all decorated with fresh or dried flowers.

In 1988, The World Powerboat Championships were held in Guernsey

One of the smallest churches in the world is in Guernsey. It is completely decorated inside and out with tiny pieces of china made into mosaics. It is called the Little Chapel and it was built by a monk.

# O what is that Sound?

O what is that sound which so thrills the ear
  Down in the valley drumming, drumming?
Only the scarlet soldiers, dear,
  The soldiers coming.

O what is that light I see flashing so clear
  Over the distance brightly, brightly?
Only the sun on their weapons, dear,
  As they step lightly.

O what are they doing with all that gear,
  What are they doing this morning, this morning?
Only their usual manoeuvres, dear
  Or perhaps a warning.

O why have they left the road down there,
    Why are they suddenly wheeling, wheeling?
Perhaps a change in their orders, dear.
    Why are you kneeling?

O haven't they stopped for the doctor's care,
    Haven't they reined their horses, their horses?
Why, they are none of them wounded, dear,
    None of these forces.

O is it the parson they want, with white hair,
    Is it the parson, is it, is it?
No, they are passing his gateway, dear,
    Without a visit.

O it must be the farmer who lives, so near.
    It must be the farmer so cunning, so cunning?
They have passed the farmyard already, dear,
    And now they are running.

O where are you going? Stay with me here!
    Were the vows you swore deceiving, deceiving?
No, I promised to love you, dear,
    But I must be leaving.

O it's broken the lock and splintered the door,
    O it's the gate where they're turning, turning;
Their boots are heavy on the floor
    And their eyes are burning.

*W. H. Auden*
*Illustrated by Azoo Design*

109

# THE WRECK OF THE BLUE BELL

It was 11 February 1877 and the good ship *Blue Bell* was steaming her way quietly into the entrance of Keppel Bay, Rockhampton in Queensland. Captain and crew would soon be safe in harbour after an uneventful voyage — or so they thought!

Suddenly, without warning, the *Blue Bell* began to rise up out of the water.

Consternation!

"A sea monster must be lifting us up!" someone gasped. They peered over the side, imagining at any minute that a huge sea serpent's head would come snaking up out of the water, ready to devour all on board. Then it became obvious what was happening! The *Blue Bell* was trapped, wedged in a crevice of rock that was slowly rising from the sea. Something supernatural? No, it was simply the result of a submarine earthquake and it was just bad luck for the captain and crew that *Blue Bell* was in the right spot at the wrong time. We're told that the ship was abandoned the next day and that the rock (now called 'Blue Bell Island') continued to rise until it was 7.6 metres above high water mark. But the records *don't* say whether anyone believed the sailors' story about how their ship ended up on top of a small hill!

# A SMALL COLLECTION OF TRAPPED WORDS

## Glossary

**adherents** *(p.38)*
people who believe strongly in an idea or cause

**appalling** *(p.39)*
dreadful

**coma** *(p.24)*
state of unconsciousness for a long time

**consigned** *(p.40)*
delivered, deposited

**barren** *(p.41)*
uninteresting, dull, lifeless

**beck** *(p.8)*
mountain stream in Northern England

**bedaubed** *(p.101)*
painted

**belligerence** *(p.39)*
being aggressive

**brands** *(p.89)*
burning sticks

**carrion** *(p.103)*
rotting meat

**contriving** *(p.79)*
managing

**decipher** *(p.41)*
interpret, make out

**disoriented** *(p.24)*
confused about the place or time, losing sense of direction

**divulge** *(p.38)*
to tell something that is secret

**erroneous** *(p.105)*
mistaken

Glossary continues on page 112

Me, friend.

Pages 110 and 111 illustrated by Michelle Smith, 12 years.

**evident** *(p.23)*
clear

**fall (the)** *(p.99)*
autumn

**fanatical** *(p.38)*
extreme

**fells** *(p.8)*
hills in Northern Britain

**frenzied** *(p.45)*
frantic, desperate

**gaunt** *(p.10)*
lean, bony, looking
desolate

**heathen** *(p.78)*
person who doesn't live
by religious principles

**pillage** *(p.78)*
to rob, often with violence

**piously** *(p.98)*
religiously

**quiver** *(p.81)*
case for holding arrows

**rational** *(p.45)*
reasonable

**rejuvenated** *(p.22)*
feeling more energetic

**replete** *(p.101)*
full

**runnels** *(p.6)*
gutters, small streams

**hysteria** *(p.18)*
uncontrollable fear or
emotion

**impertinent** *(p.39)*
rude, not showing respect

**intently** *(p.47)*
in a concentrated way

**janitor** *(p.96)*
caretaker

**lamenting** *(p.13)*
mournful, distressed

**ludicrous** *(p.43)*
silly

**meridian** *(p.19)*
highest point in the sky

**munitions** *(p.105)*
weapons and ammunition

**mustered** *(p.90)*
gathered

**sanctuary** *(p.46)*
refuge, safe place

**sedately** *(p.45)*
quietly and slowly

**sexton** *(p.67)*
caretaker of church and
churchyard (could
include bell-ringing or
grave-digging)

**smith** *(p.78)*
person who works with
metal

**sulfa** *(p.98)*
a substance used in
medicine

**taut** *(p.18)*
tight, strained, tense

**terse** *(p.42)*
short-tempered, snappy

**ultimately** *(p.89)*
in the end